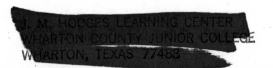

A PROFESSIONAL GUIDE TO COMMODITY SPECULATION

A PROFESSIONAL GUIDE TO COMMODITY SPECULATION

John E. B. Shaw

PARKER PUBLISHING COMPANY, INC.   WEST NYACK, N.Y.

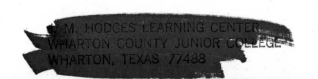

Executive Success Library Edition . . . . . . September 1979

For my wife

LAURA

whose first experience in the commodity
markets was to be handed a delivery
notice—and a bill—for *forty-five thousand
dozen eggs!*

WHAT THIS BOOK CAN DO FOR YOU

After you have read through this book for the first time, you will have useful knowledge of all phases of commodity futures trading, whether it be for speculation, hedging or investment.

You will know if this increasingly popular type of money-handling is for you.

A second reading will help you decide what type of commodity futures trading you wish to do.

Speculation is fascinating to most of us and a wealth of material is submitted for your critical inspection which, in turn, could challenge you to explore or develop your own speculative programs.

You will want to know how to use the seasonal markets where advantage can be taken of the price trends of the crops as they are grown, harvested and used.

The futures markets for perishables such as cattle, hogs, bellies and eggs tend to run in cyclical swings. Good profits can be achieved if these swings are estimated correctly.

Often, one commodity will be too expensive or too cheap in relation to another commodity which may be substituted for it. Spreading, which tries to take advantage of this price imbalance, is thoroughly discussed and many profitable spreads are analyzed together with suggestions as to when to spread and when not to do so.

Every speculator and investor has heard about charting and many have made charts almost a life study. This book gives you an introduction to this popular method of attempting to forecast the future by reading the footprints of the past. Bar charting and point and figure charting are both covered in considerable detail.

In our computer age, we tend to use mechanical methods and computers to solve a myriad of problems. The commodity markets are no exception; countless mechanical methods and computer techniques have been adapted to profitably estimate the ebb and flow of these markets. In this book, several usually successful mechanical methods are given in detail and other attacks on this problem are suggested. A summary of a two and one-half year study of one computer method is also given, together with suggestions on the further use of the computer in these commodity markets.

Every trader should know that hedging is an important part of every commodity market. This is a fact that is frequently overlooked by the public. A careful explanation of the hedging function is given and several examples of how to take advantage of hedging are outlined.

For the investor, the commodity markets represent an almost untouched field, yet commodities can be a very good investment indeed. Large profits can be made by the patient investor who recognizes the cyclical nature of almost every commodity. One of the earliest chapters in the book delves into these opportunities in detail and a later one shows you how to use the Dow Jones Commodity Futures Index as a trading guide.

The investor may not be as active in the markets as the speculator. He may have only two or three trades a year but these may be highly profitable and often represent long term capital gains which are taxed at a lower rate.

The mention of taxes brings the reader to the book's discussion of taxes and tax straddles. Even if you are entirely wedded to stocks or real estate to achieve your capital gains, it is useful to know a short term capital gain of any kind may often be converted into a long term capital gain, taxable at a lower rate, through the use of commodity tax straddles. This is one of the fastest growing uses of the commodity markets and it can only be because many persons have found the advantage of such tax straddles.

I should also add that, unless otherwise stated, prices quoted are closing prices and dates are the date specified or its nearest neighbor. Although statistics and prices in this book have been carefully checked, using authoritative sources wherever possible, the author cannot assume responsibility for their interpretation and use. I recommend that you discuss your objectives with a professional commodity broker.

When you have read this book through twice, put it down, think about what it has told you and place it where you can refer to it often. The lessons of the past are valuable to us only to the degree we use them to profit in the future.

John E. B. Shaw

ACKNOWLEDGMENTS

I was born into a family of commodity brokers. My grandfather and my father were members of The Chicago Board of Trade when that institution and the New York Stock Exchange were *the* markets of the country. There is a family story, no doubt apocryphal, that my father took me down into the wheat pit when I was four months old and, in my swaddling clothes, I was handed from broker to broker all around the pit until I arrived back in my father's arms clutching a bright, new penny. My first commodity profit!

Naturally, my first job was in the brokerage business where I stayed throughout the depression. In 1935, I entered the pharmaceutical manufacturing business where I remained until 1958 when I sold out and returned to my first love, the commodity and stock markets.

When someone is in love, they want to tell the world about it and, thus, I began teaching a course in Commodity Trading at the Denver Extension of the University of Colorado in 1966.

I had my lecture notes for the course mimeographed for my students but did not think of doing anything more about them until a good friend, John Hurlbut, suggested I expand them into this book.

I soon found out that a book is the joint effort of many people. After the manuscript was typed, I sent it off to my good friend, Robert L. Martin, who is past Chairman of the Chicago Board of Trade. Mr. Martin gave me many constructive suggestions which sharpened the book's accuracy and made it more readable.

Then, I found that although I had a good deal of theory on the subject of animal and poultry feeding, I had little practical experience. With the help of another good friend, Prof. Liston Leyendecker of Colorado State University, a liaison was established with two experts, Prof. Howard L. Enos and Prof. Marvin W. Heeney, of that institution. I am grateful for their help.

After many years of hearing the United States Department of Agriculture alternately praised and damned, I had the pleasant experience of meeting several of its officials here in Denver and want to thank them for their efforts in my behalf.

The clearest and most complete commodity charts I could find are published by the Commodity Research Bureau, Inc. and I am pleased permission was given to reproduce a number of them. Morgan, Rogers & Roberts, Inc. also allowed me to reproduce a chart on Point & Figure Tops and Bottoms in the chapter on that subject.

The Dow Jones Commodity Futures Index, which I quote extensively in the chapter entitled "How to Trade on the Futures Index," is published by Dow Jones & Company, Inc. and is to my mind as important to commodity traders as the better known Dow Jones Industrial Index is to the stock broker.

And, finally, for her zealous work in annotating, correcting, typing and retyping this manuscript, I want to thank one dear person in particular!

CONTENTS

TABLES

FIGURES

A PROFESSIONAL GUIDE TO
COMMODITY SPECULATION

THE INVESTMENT ADVANTAGE OF COMMODITIES OVER STOCKS

Let's think for a moment about the difference between stocks and commodities. Had you bought and held any one of a thousand "hot" stocks back in 1960, you would have very little left of your investment today. Had you sold IBM short in 1960 and maintained your short position over the years, you would probably be broke by now. In other words, stocks have a habit of going into a long term trend, either up or down, and not reversing that trend for many years, if at all. A losing company usually loses money until it is bankrupt while a winning management in a vigorous industry goes on and on to new heights with only occasional interruptions in its upward trend.

Commodities are different. Why? *Because commodities usually return to a profitable price.*

What do I mean by that? I mean that if you were to buy or sell short an actively traded commodity future today, sooner or later you would make a profit on that trade or its accrued successors.

To prove this statement that *commodities usually return to a profitable price,* we will examine the fluctuations of wheat between October 1963 and July 1966. We will buy September wheat at the *highest price* it registered and see how long it takes to make a profit. See Illustration 1-1.

Year	Date	Trade	Price	¢ Profit	¢ Loss
1964	1-6	Bought September wheat	181 1/8		
1964	8-28	Sold September wheat	144		37 1/8
		Bought July wheat	149 1/4		
1965	6-29	Sold July wheat	140 7/8		8 3/8
		Bought May wheat	150 3/8		
1966	4-28	Sold May wheat	159	8 5/8	
		Bought March wheat	167 3/8		
1966	9-14	Sold March wheat	206 3/4	39 3/8	

Illustration 1-1

This gives us a gross profit of 2 1/2 cents ($125). Deduct total commissions of $88 and you have a net profit of $37 on these transactions.

A tiny recompense for two and three-quarter years of waiting? Certainly, but how many stocks that were on the market three years ago have almost vanished from the quotation sheets, leaving the investor with an almost worthless certificate and no chance to recoup?

Of course, if you had sold short at 181 1/8 instead of buying, you would have had a handsome profit fairly soon.

Remember, we bought at the highest price that September 1964 wheat reached during its entire crop year.

I have given you this tabulation right at the start of this book because I wanted to prove to you by actual market performance that this statement of mine had validity. There is little point in reading this book unless you can trust its prices and honor its statements.

So, remember this most important factor in commodity trading:

Commodities usually return to a profitable price.

HOW TO EVALUATE COMMODITIES
AS INVESTMENTS

One of the things which irritates a commodity broker is he is sometimes regarded as a second class citizen by the high and mighty stockbroker. Even the hustling mutual fund tribe consider him something less than human while the average investment banker in his pin-striped suit tries to imagine the whole commodity complex doesn't really exist at all.

I've had it happen to me.

"This is Mr. Shaw," I am introduced in a bright tone. Then in a lower register, "He deals in commodities."

I'm sure the same low decibels would be used if I dealt in women.

Of course, this may all be a put-up job by the stock houses, especially those who can't or won't see the real value behind a commodity future. Some may rather sell you a thousand shares of some electronics-mobile home-pollution control-candy manufacturing conglomerate, whose president may be a bum, aided by a treasurer who can't add and a sales manager whose best deals are with blondes in a dark bar. That's a legitimate company, that is, not a messy, slippery deal like commodities.

Yet, commodities can be a very good investment indeed. Far, far better than most stocks; in fact, so much better that I am always shocked by the lack of public appreciation of their investment possibilities.

Of course, when I am talking about investments, I am addressing myself to those who want to see their capital grow. I am not talking to those who want a safe 6 percent per annum on their money and little or no risk. Also, commodity futures cannot be used for a loan at the bank in case of emergency so you should have enough spare capital to see you through life's other little crises. That way you won't have to cash in your futures at the wrong time just to get eating money.

Remember what I said at the start of this book?

Commodities usually return to a profitable price.
I will now add a corollary: **Unlike many, many stocks!**

In my very first chapter, I showed you that even if you had bought wheat at the highest price of the crop year, you would have ended up with a profit. What, therefore, would you have made if instead of buying it that year at its high, you had bought wheat near its low? You know the answer; a very good profit would have been yours, well over 100 percent on a short term investment.

For the rest of this chapter, we are going to use a technique I have devised to buy a commodity near its low and try to make 100 percent on our average investment.

Commodity prices usually rise and fall like irregular waves; a shortage is usually followed by a glut which is followed by another shortage, all with appropriate price variations. So we want to buy in time of glut—or semi-glut—preferably when all are saying that more glut is on the way.

How to buy at that time? Let's take the price history of a future over the past five years and analyze its price range.

It is June, 1969, and we are looking at the wheat market. The high and low on May wheat for the previous five years has been (Illustration 2-1):

	High	Low
1964-65	163 1/4	142 3/4
1965-66	173	147
1966-67	207	160
1967-68	187 1/2	132 5/8
1968-69	153 1/2	125 1/8

Illustration 2-1

So, we have a five year range of 207 to 125 1/8, an extreme difference of 81 7/8 cents between high and low.

Divide that difference by 3 which gives us roughly 27 1/4 cents, and by using that figure we divide the five year price structure into three areas (Illustration 2-2):

1st Third	207	– 179 3/4
2nd Third	179 5/8	– 152 1/2
3rd Third	152 3/8	– 125 1/8

Illustration 2-2

As our purpose is to buy in times of low prices only, our rule will be that we only do so when we can get a price within the bottom third of any five year history.

Using this rule, we were able to buy May 1970 wheat futures at 141 1/8 the first day they were traded on June 2, 1969. We put up $500 per contract margin and sat back to see what would happen. In July, the futures hit a low of 129 1/4 which meant we were out 12 cents and needed additional margin of $600 per contract which we put up. Our investment was now $1,100 per contract. By November, prices had recovered to our purchase level and we got our additional margin back so we had that $1,100 up for five months.

On April 29, 1970, the last day we could hold the May future without risking delivery, we were able to sell it for 151 5/8, making a net profit of $503 per contract.

We had an average investment of approximately $773 during that time ($1,100 for five months and $500 for six), so we made about 65 percent on our investment in eleven months.

But we want 100 percent on our money! With that idea sticking in our brain, we analyze the previous five years on March 1971 wheat (Illustration 2-3).

	High	Low
1965-66	173	147
1966-67	207 1/4	160 1/2
1967-68	193 1/2	144 7/8
1968-69	164 1/4	123 3/4
1969-70	154 1/4	129 1/4

Illustration 2-3

This gives us a five year range of 207 1/4 to 123 3/4 for a difference of 83 1/2 cents between the highest and lowest prices. Again, we divide it into thirds (Illustration 2-4):

1st Third	207 1/4 − 179 1/2
2nd Third	179 3/8 − 151 5/8
3rd Third	151 1/2 − 123 3/4

Illustration 2-4

The price of March 1971 wheat on April 29, 1970, was 152 3/8 to 151 1/4, just barely at our bottom third. We determine to buy at 151 3/8 or better and do so on May 1.

Now, to adjust our sights. We want to make 100 percent on our total investment. If March wheat will go to 162 and we don't get a margin call in the meantime, we will do it. On June 8, however, it sold down to 142 1/2 and we are called for $450 additional margin so our total investment is now $950.

However, the price recovers and by the middle of July we are able to withdraw $200, leaving $750 as margin as the exchange has raised its requirements to 15 cents per contract.

We have had $500 up for a little over a month and $950 up for another month for an average investment of $725 for the two and one-half months and now we have to keep it at $750. This changes our price objective of 100 percent on our money to 151 1/4 + 15 + 5/8 cents commission or a total of 166 7/8.

We achieve this on August 17, 1970, having held the contract a little over three and one-half months.

Let's recapitulate. Using our lowest-third price theory, we have been in the wheat market almost continuously from June 2, 1969, to August 17, 1970. Our greatest investment was $1,100 and our net profits totaled $503 + $751 = $1,254 or about 114 percent on our largest capital requirement and we did this in less than 15 months.

Now, admittedly, all the above is hindsight and we didn't really make those trades; we were merely testing out a theory. Also, please remember, when we are dealing with price supported commodities, like grains, we are in more dangerous territory due to changing support levels than when we are dealing in cocoa, sugar or the metals.

For instance, Chicago wheat had an equivalent support price of $2.00 or over for some years. It is now $1.50. Manifestly, if you had bought at even the lowest third in the $2.00 area, you would have had a much longer wait for a profit when the support price was dropped to about $1.50 in 1964, although the actual futures price went back above $2.00 in 1966.

Here is another statistical example (Illustration 2-5):

Maine Potatoes (May delivery)

	High	Low
1964-65	6.50	2.83
1965-66	5.33	3.40
1966-67	4.82	1.81
1967-68	3.94	1.95
1968-69	4.26	2.30

Five year range: 6.50 − 1.81, difference 4.69

1st Third	6.50 − 4.94
2nd Third	4.93 − 3.38
3rd Third	3.37 − 1.81

Illustration 2-5

The original margin on potatoes at this price is $300 (60 points), commission is about 6 points. Since we want to try to make 100 percent on our money, we set a profit objective of 66 points.

May 1970 potatoes went on the board the first of June but it was not until June 9, 1969, that they came down to our upper price limit of 3.37, where we bought them. On October 10, they reached a low of 2.99 and we had to put up 38 x $5 = $190 more margin, making our investment $490.

However, the market quickly recovered and we got our $190 back by October 23, when the price rose to 3.37 again.

On December 2, 1969, we sold out at 4.02 for our 66 point gain. It had taken us six months to make 100 percent on our money, not counting in that 100 percent the two weeks in October when we had to pony up that extra $190.

Going through the price sheets over the years, I can see many such situations and also many where short sales in the top third of the price range would have been profitable. The only things wrong with a short sale for investment purposes are they are always regarded as short-term by the federal tax men and the sky may be the limit on your losses while you are waiting for that almost inevitable day when the market collapses of its own weight and you go into the profit column.

Another way you might use this price theory is to buy only if you can obtain a price in the lower *sixth* of the scale (Illustration 2-6):

July Soybean Oil

	High	Low
1964-65	12.35	9.12
1965-66	13.10	8.82
1966-67	12.70	8.78
1967-68	9.61	7.00
1968-69	8.66	7.22

Five year range: 13.10 − 7.00, difference 6.10.

1st Sixth	13.10 − 12.09
2nd Sixth	12.08 − 11.07
3rd Sixth	11.06 − 10.05
4th Sixth	10.04 − 9.03
5th Sixth	9.02 − 8.01
6th Sixth	8.00 − 7.00

Illustration 2-6

Using the lowest sixth method, we bought July 1970 soybean oil at 7.44 on July 30, 1969, the first day it was traded. To achieve our 100 percent profit, we need to make back our margin of $300 (50 points) plus commissions of $30 (5 points), 7.44 + 55 = 7.99.

We get our profit on September 25, and could have had 200 percent by October 24. The lowest price reached after our purchase was 7.35, so we were never called for more margin.

Buying in the bottom sixth has several advantages. You know you are buying at an out-of-line price and also your chance of making 100 or even 200 percent on your investment is greatly enhanced. However, that profit may sometimes be a long time in coming.

Say it is July, 1968, and we have spotted a lower sixth situation (Illustration 2-7):

Accordingly, on July 19, 1968, we buy March corn at 121 5/8, putting up $500 margin. On September 30, the price makes a low of 106. To margin it down to about this point, we have had to make additional deposits totaling about $780, so now our investment is $1,280.

March Corn

	High	Low
1963-64	129	114 3/8
1964-65	131 1/4	117
1965-66	131	118
1966-67	158 5/8	123 1/4
1967-68	148 3/4	116 1/4

Five year range: 158 5/8 — 114 3/8, difference 44 1/4.

1st Sixth	158 5/8 — 151 3/8
2nd Sixth	151 1/4 — 144
3rd Sixth	143 7/8 — 136 5/8
4th Sixth	136 1/2 — 129 1/4
5th Sixth	129 1/8 — 121 3/4
6th Sixth	121 5/8 — 114 3/8

Illustration 2-7

We sell out our March delivery on February 27, 1969, at 114 1/8 for a loss of 7 1/2 cents plus about 1/2 cent commissions. We also get back about $280 of our additional margin. Our deposit is now $1,000.

Immediately, we buy December 1969 corn at 115 3/8 and sell this out on November 26 at 119 1/8 for a profit of 3 3/4 cents less about 1/2 cent commissions. We withdraw our $165 profit and now have a margin deposit of $835.

The same day, we buy September 1970 corn at 125 1/4. On February 9, 1970, it touches 120 1/8 and we have to put up another $250. We now have $1,085 in our margin account and decide to refigure our profit needs in the light of all the additional margin we have shuffled back and forth. We figure our average deposit has been about $1,100. Also, we still have a net loss of about $238 on our transactions to date.

If we are to make 100 percent on our margin average of $1,100, equivalent to 22 cents, plus recouping our losses of $238, about 4 3/4 cents, we must sell our September corn at a 27 3/8 cents profit, from which would be deducted about 5/8 cent commission, new scale.

Glory be, we attain this price of 152 5/8 cents on August 18, 1970. In fact, we would have had a bonus as it opened at 158 3/4 but since this is only a statistical study, we will not labor the point.

It has taken us a little over two years to make 100 percent on our average margin. This shows that you may have to wait for awhile before cashing in those lower sixth "chips" but that eventually they should have solid value.

Remember, too, you are always flying in the face of "experience" when you buy in the lower sixth. It is a time of almost universal gloom about the price of the commodity in question. Everyone is either planting it or breeding it or mining it, the boys in the Street say it's going much lower, the chart looks terrible and, altogether, the situation is going to the devil. That's when you take a hard look at the bottom sixth, dear readers, and prepare to loosen your purse strings. The price may go lower, it usually does, but it will also usually recover. I remember when cocoa hit 20 cents in 1965, I thought it was dirt cheap historically. It was but it went down below 10 cents before it recovered to sell at 48 cents only four years later.

Some may say you are losing interest on your margin money by having it up for so long a period of time. But I would rather take a good chance of making 50 to 200 percent on it than to be guaranteed a nice, safe 5 percent on my *risk*—or speculative— capital.

3

HOW TO GET INTO THE
COMMODITY MARKETS

Almost all speculative trading on the commodity markets is in futures contracts. A futures contract means just what it says. If you buy a contract, you agree to take delivery of a certain amount of that commodity at a specified future time. For instance, you buy one contract (5,000 bushels) of July wheat. This means that you are assuming the responsibility of having 5,000 bushels of wheat delivered to you some time in July. Of course, the wheat won't be dumped at your office door, you'll merely get a warehouse receipt showing that you own 5,000 bushels of wheat. The only way to eliminate this delivery is to sell out your wheat contract before delivery is made to you, thus shifting the burden of taking delivery to the man to whom you sell the contract.

Conversely, if you sell short one contract of July wheat, you are saying that you will deliver 5,000 bushels of wheat to the buyer during July. The only way you can escape doing this is to cancel your contract by buying in your short sale. Of course, you rarely buy in or sell out your wheat contract with the person who first traded it to you. It is just necessary that you shift the responsibility for delivery problems to another speculator.

All commodity exchanges use a monthly delivery structure for futures trading whether it be March corn, May wheat or July pork bellies.

Throughout this book, I will be quoting prices; wheat at $1.49, cotton at 23.25, sugar at 3.46 and so on. These prices will always indicate cost per unit of measurement. Grains and soybeans are measured in bushels; cotton, sugar, soybean oil, pork bellies, cattle, hogs and many others are priced by the pound. Some commodities have different units of measurement, soybean meal, for example, is priced on a per ton basis while silver and platinum are quoted by the ounce. You should find out the unit of measurement *and* the size of your contract before making any commitment in the futures market.

To those who are accustomed to the more staid and solid New York Stock Exchange, the floor behavior and discipline of the average commodity exchange comes as quite a shock. All that noise and confusion! How can they know what they are doing?

Yet the commodity exchanges for all their seeming pandemonium get the job of trading done in an efficient and accurate manner. As the son and grandson of members of the Chicago Board of Trade, I would also say that the standard of business morality of the average member there is fully as high as that of a member of the New York Stock Exchange.

Having delivered myself of that praise, I will proceed to the homily, the cautionary message.

First, remember that a membership on the leading commodity exchanges is quite expensive, usually much more than the price of a seat on the New York Stock Exchange. The growth of commodity trading has consistently pushed the cost of these memberships higher and higher.

Second, you have the fact that the average member of a commodity exchange does a lot more trading for his own account than a member of a stock exchange. This is because he can do this at almost no commission expense. "Day trading" in which you make and close out your commitment the same day costs you, the non-member speculator on the Chicago Board of Trade, about $20 per contract or over 3/8 cent. However, the member trading in the pit only has to pay from $1.60 to $3.00 as a clearing fee, which at $3.00 is less than 1/16 cent. It can be highly profitable, as you can see, for the pit trader to even make eighths since the profit of 1/8 cent on a day trade means $6.25 − $3.00 or $3.25 per contract. Do this on enough contracts per day and you have a comfortable living, even after losses.

Of course, the average pit trader does no such thing. He is usually just like any other speculator, trying to gauge the market correctly and being wrong more often than he is right. As my father used to say to me when the subject of pit traders came up,

"If they are so darned smart, why are they screaming their heads off every day for a fee of a couple of dollars a trade?"

Third, many times an otherwise active market becomes dull and listless. The trading public is waiting to see which way the cat is going to jump. Floor traders sense that there are a number of "stop" orders above or below the market which will be activated by a good day's move in either direction. At this time, individual traders on the floor may attempt to force a situation, to raise or depress the price to a point where the stop orders are activated. This process known as "gunning for stops" can be very rewarding. They can sell the market down to where the public's sell stops are activated. At this point they turn from sellers to buyers, buying up the sell stop orders at a profit and also buying new contracts at the low price level. In the absence of their selling, the market slowly returns to its former price level. They then sell out the contracts bought at the lower prices and rest content. They have made two profits; one on their short sales used to depress the market to the stop points where they buy in and go long and, the second, when they sell out their cheap longs as the market recovers to its normal price.

How do they get away with this? First, it's not illegal; the individual traders are risking their own money in the hope they have gauged the market correctly. Other traders may take the opposite side; they buy all the contracts that are offered for sale and then run the market up to the point where the first group have to cover their short sales at a substantial loss.

Also, when you are talking about the commodity exchanges, you are usually not talking about real *money*. The margin on a million bushels of wheat is about one hundred thousand dollars. Five hundred shares of IBM which takes only a fraction of a second to print on the New York Stock Exchange tape is worth over a hundred thousand dollars. Yet the trader who has a million bushels of wheat in his account is a big customer on the Chicago Board of Trade while on the New York Stock Exchange he is just another guy named Joe.

So, while many have made and lost large sums on the commodity exchanges, such is not the rule. The average commodity trader I know has about $5,000 in his account, equivalent to less than 20 shares of IBM at 1970 values. However, he can get a lot more action for his $5,000 in the commodity markets than he can from even as volatile a stock as IBM.

Of course, to illustrate my point, I may have over-emphasized the role of the speculative floor traders. Most of the time they are going about their normal business, buying and selling for their customers. It is only when a situation starts to look ripe to their sensitive trading antennas that they begin to take more than a general interest in the state of that particular market.

All U.S. Commodity Exchanges are regulated and supervised by The Commodity Futures Trading Commission, commonly known as the CFTC. This body of 5 men, assisted by a battery of legal and financial aides is an official branch of the U.S. Government and with very broad powers over all phases of commodity trading. While it has had the usual teething troubles of a new agency, it is just now really beginning to assert its powers. In reality, I hope that it will become to the commodity markets, what the S.E.C. is to the stock markets.

One of the actions taken by the CFTC and much applauded by many brokers was the discontinuance of the sale of commodity "calls." Most of these calls were written against foreign markets, although some had no backing at all. The CFTC may allow "put" and "call" sales in the future but I believe that such activities will be closely supervised.

Bear in mind, however, that the CFTC has absolutely no powers over the antics of foreign commodity markets and that you enter such markets without the umbrella of its protection.

With the great growth of commodity trading, all exchanges have become much more sensitive to their public images since any injury to that image can result in a decline of dollar volume of business. Yet, some of them, in my opinion, have a long way to go in that direction.

Of course, the average speculator never gets on or even near the floor of the exchange which is handling his business. He is dependent upon his broker to see that he gets a good price on his trades.

All right, then, how well should you know your broker? In this age of telephone solicitation, many traders only know him as a disembodied voice over the phone. Yet this fellow is handling your money in many situations and it would appear to me you should know him better than you do your barber. (Some unhappy speculators insist he *was* their barber only in a different way!) I have a warm phone relationship with some people I have seldom seen but I also have lost some good accounts which I am sure I could have held had they been close enough for me to have better understood their aims and personalities.

So, try to maintain at least occasional physical encounters with your broker, times when you can sit down and quietly talk over the past and future of your account with him.

To conclude this chapter, I will give you a number of rules which I ask you to *never* disregard:

1. Use only mental stops *and stick to them.* Do not put in a stop order unless the market is very near your price. Just buy or sell at the market if the price hits your mental stop.

2. Know your broker and his brokerage firm. It does not have to be a New York Stock Exchange member but it should be a substantial one or a small firm with lots of capital. Remember, there is usually *no* guaranty fund to protect the customers of *any* failed commodity firm although congressional efforts along that line are presently being made.

3. Pick an experienced commodity broker, preferably one you have met. The experienced broker will usually ask you how much money you can put into the commodity markets as risk capital. If it is less than $5,000, he will often tell you to buy a mutual fund or a utility stock. He knows that a fellow with only $2,000, or so, operating on those 7 to 10 percent commodity margins is not going to have a chance, usually, to do anything but lose.

4. Only commit 50 percent of your operating capital at any one time. That way you can survive market mishaps and still stay in the game.

5. Trade only in big volume commodities. These markets are large enough to prevent manipulation and you will also not be skinned by a big difference between bid and asked prices.

6. Try to stick to United States exchanges. It may be fascinating to trade on Paris and London but you know nothing about the rules and regulations, if any, of those exchanges and that lack may be costly.

7. Have a trading plan that has proved profitable in the past. If you can't make money on paper, you certainly are going to have a hard time doing it when real cash is involved.

8. Think independently. Avoid the "herd" instinct. The herd is often wrong.

4

HOW TO TAKE ADVANTAGE
OF HEDGING

Hedging is the only reason for having a commodity futures market. Without its facilities for hedging, any such market merely becomes a Las Vegas without the girls.

Hedging is an insurance policy for the producer and user and a very valuable policy it can sometimes be!

Let's take a look at basic wheat farm finance.

Each year, the farmer is given a wheat acreage allotment by the government. He can use only this acreage on which to grow wheat. If his wheat acreage exceeds the allotment, he is not eligible for loan or certificate payments.

The wheat he grows on this allotment can be converted into cash in two ways: he can sell it or he can put it into government loan. If he does the latter, he will get the local loan price for it and, in effect, give the government a chattel mortgage on his wheat. If he wishes to withdraw it from the loan, he must pay back the amount the government advanced plus storage and interest. If he does not redeem it within a certain period, the government takes over the wheat in payment for the loan.

In addition, the farmer gets a certificate payment. In 1969, in Colorado, this was 43 percent of his allotment times his yield times $1.52/bu.

How does the government ascertain this certificate payment rate? It is the difference between the national average loan rate and parity as of July 1 of the harvest year. In 1969, parity was $2.77 and the national average loan rate was $1.25.

What is parity? It is the amount that wheat is worth in relation to the prices the farmer has to pay for goods and services now, based on 1910-1914 figures.

Who pays the cost of these certificates? The millers remit 75 cents/bu. to the government on each bushel of wheat ground by them for domestic use only. The remainder is paid by the Treasury Department.

Now for a practical example of hedging.

You own a farm in Weld County, Colorado. It is January, 1969, and you expect the wheat grown on your 400 acre allotment to be well over 10,000 bushels. However, you also know very well that if you sell your wheat at the cash price when you harvest it in July, you are barely going to make ends meet even with the certificate payments bringing part of your return up to parity. The loan price is also too low for comfort. A way out of this bind might be to try to make a little more money by hedging your crop. Wheat is usually seasonally higher in January than in July.

You call a broker and find that the hedging margin on wheat is $300 per 5,000 bushel contract. On January 10, you sell 10,000 bushels of July wheat short in Kansas City, obtaining a price of $1.34 1/2. You also send your broker $600 to margin your trade.

On June 30, your crop is nearing harvest. It will only make about 10,000 bushels which you plan to sell to the elevator at the cash price of about $1.10. You also call your broker and tell him to cover your short sale of 10,000 bushels which he does at $1.23 1/2. Your profit on this trade is $1,100 minus $44 commission or $1,056. This is what you have made by using the hedging facilities of the futures market. In effect, you have insured yourself so that you would get a certain price for your wheat. True, $1,056, is not a great deal of money but in a farming operation of your size it can make all the difference.

Let's calculate: you received $1.10/bu. from the elevator for your 10,000 bushels. That's $11,000. You also will receive an allotment payment of 43 percent x 400 acres x 25 bu. yield x $1.52 = $6,536. Your total income on your wheat will thus be $17,536 or $1.75/bu. Add your hedging profit to this and you get $18,592 or $1.85/bu., a gain of 10 cents/bu.

This example, which they all know, should be enough to convince the farmers they should hedge but, strangely enough, few of them do so. They either rely on the loan price or contract to sell their crop to a user or just play it by ear and hope the overworked Almighty will hear their prayers for $2.00 wheat. Of course, the big corporate farms hedge their crops when it pays to do so and rely on the loan when prices are not high enough.

You should remember, too, that if prices rise contra-seasonally and the price is higher in July than in January, you would lose on your futures contract but gain all or some of your loss back by being able to sell your actual wheat for a higher cash price.

So, the insurance policy works both ways. Here's an example:

In January

You sell July futures at $1.50.

In July

You buy in your futures at $1.25.
You sell your cash wheat at $1.20.

Result: You have made 25 cents per bushel so you have actually sold your wheat for $1.45, not $1.20.

In January

You sell futures at $1.50.

In July

You buy in your futures at $1.75.
You sell your cash wheat for $1.70.

Result: You have lost 25 cents per bushel on your futures but actually have sold your wheat for $1.45 ($1.70 − 0.25 = $1.45).

Like all insurance policies, there is a limitation on the protection hedging can buy you. Also, like the majority of casualty policies, they can often seem to be a waste of money. In the first example, hedging has paid off by limiting your loss; in the second, it has limited your profit.

As I have said, some years the price is so low it is hard for the farmer to hedge at a profit. But even in this type of market, there is a large amount of hedging.

Example: You are running a flour mill and you contract to sell the flour you can mill from 5,000 bushels of wheat. Delivery is to be in two months at the *present* price of flour.

You don't know what the price of wheat is going to be in two months but you have contracted to sell the flour based on today's wheat prices. You have to hedge the flour sale, thus:

Today	Two Months from Today
You sell the flour based on today's cash price of $1.50 for wheat.	You buy cash wheat to make the flour at $1.55.
You also buy 5,000 bushels of wheat futures at $1.65	You sell your futures contract for $1.70.

Thus, while the wheat for the flour has cost you 5 cents per bushel more than you figured, the profit in the futures trade has made up that loss so you were able to quote a profitable price for flour two months in advance of your actual purchase of the wheat you will use to grind the flour.

Here is the real point to hedging: *If the producer or user could not hedge his commodity in the futures market, the prices paid by everyone would be much higher.*

If you had not been able to hedge your flour sale, for instance, you would have been forced to add about 10 cents per bushel to your quoted price for that flour, just to insure your firm against taking a loss when you had to actually buy the wheat to make that flour. The existence of a hedging market made that added expense unnecessary and, thus, helped to hold down the price the housewife had to pay when she bought that flour in the supermarket.

Now, admittedly, this is a once over lightly on the hedging sector of the market. Since I am writing this book for speculators, I will not go further into the intricacies of hedging. It is just necessary for everyone to know that the hedger is always present in every futures market. Indeed, he and the speculator *are* the market.

5

WHY COMMODITY MARGINS
ARE NEEDED

Margin money is your earnest money. It is your deposit with your broker as a guarantee against loss in your account. Margins are not set arbitrarily by your broker. They are set by the Governors of each individual commodity exchange or its clearing house. They are not set by the government. When volume is low, margins tend to be low. When trading increases and price changes get a little wilder, margins begin to go up. This takes place for two reasons:

1. To protect the exchange members against large price changes due to increased volume. That is, to protect them against their customers not being able to pay their bills.
2. To discourage over-speculation by limiting the amount you can trade per dollar of margin money.

The margins set by the exchange must be observed by all its members. This is not just talk. The exchange's clearing house balances all trades daily. If we are a member house with a net long position of a million bushels of wheat and the margin is $500 per 5,000 bushels, we as a firm must deposit $100,000 as margin with the clearing house to protect the other firms that sold the wheat to us.

We obtain this $100,000 from our customers whose individual positions add up to our million bushels of long wheat. Thus, the margin money you put up is in turn pledged by the firm to the clearing house as its margin.

Of course, there is a slight gimmick here. If you are long 5,000 bushels and I am short 5,000 bushels with the same house, we would both have to put up $500 with the broker but as the two trades offset each other, the broker would not have to put up anything with the clearing house. However, he must have this deposit from each of us to protect him against loss in our individual accounts.

The only times that margins may vary from customer-to-customer or house-to-house are usually three:

1. Hedging margins are usually lower than speculative margins.
2. Spreading (straddling) margins between deliveries or between related commodities

are almost invariably lower than those demanded for the same number of outright long or short positions.

3. Large wire houses may ask higher margins than the exchange miminums. They do this to help their customers protect themselves from the dangers of overtrading on their capital.

Now, that we have taken note of the philosophy and mechanics of margins, we had better learn how to figure them.

First, remember there are two kinds of margin, *original* and *maintenance*. Original margin is the amount you have to put up when you initiate your trade. Maintenance margin means what it says, it is the amount of your original margin less your on-paper loss that must be maintained before you are called for more margin. *A call is usually for the amount necessary to restore your margin on the trade to its original amount.*

Let's look at a typical example:

Regular wheat contract = 5,000 bushels
Each cent of price change = $50 (5,000 x $0.01 = $50)
Original margin requirements = $500 (10 cents)
Maintenance margin required = $350 (7 cents)

Thus, if we buy long or sell short one contract of wheat we must deposit $500 with the broker as earnest money.

Three things then can happen:

1. If the market goes against us and we have a paper loss of 2 1/2 cents ($125) we do not need to put up more margin as we are still above maintenance. $500 − 125 = $375. Maintenance $350. Excess over maintenance is $25.

2. If the market goes against us 4 cents ($200), we will be below maintenance. $500 − 200 = $300. Maintenance $350. Additional margin which must be deposited is $200. $500 − 300 = $200.

3. If the market goes our way and we have a profit of 5 cents ($250), then we can use that money as part margin on another contract or even withdraw it from our account. Most people leave it in until the transaction is closed, however. Do you get the margin idea? Do you know how to figure them? Be sure you do, it can be of vital importance to you.

Now, a few comments on margins.

First, commissions are never figured into margins due since the clearing house which is the source of all margin requirements is never involved in brokers' commissions.

Second, margins are much too low. I advise my customers to never let their original margins start below 25 percent of their outstanding trades. Thus, if we own 10,000 bushels of wheat selling at $1.50 per bushel, we have bought $15,000 worth of wheat. I try to have margin deposits of $3,750 on this instead of the $1,000 to $1,500 asked by the clearing house. My reason for doing so is graphically outlined in my second chapter. Please re-read it if you've forgotten what it said.

Third, margins are figured on your overall account. If you are out $250 on wheat which would put you below maintenance but have a profit of $300 on corn, that profit would cancel out your wheat loss and you would not be called for more margin on it.

Fourth, do not pyramid positions. Pyramiding is the process of using paper profits to buy more of the same commodity without putting up any more hard cash. You have bought four contracts of wheat at $1.60. Thus, every cent wheat goes up you have $200 profit. (4 x 5,000 = 20,000 x $0.01 = $200.) Wheat goes to $1.68. You have $1,600 paper profit. Instead of taking it you buy three more contracts using your profit for margin. $500 margin per contract times three equals $1,500. You now have seven contracts. Wheat goes to $1.71. Your profit is now $2,650, or $1,050 more than it was. You use $1,000 of this to buy two more contracts at $1.71. You now have nine contracts. Wheat goes to $1.72. Your profit is now $3,100 or $450 more than you had. You use this $450 plus the $50 excess from last time to buy one more contract of wheat at $1.72. You now have ten contracts and every cent wheat goes up or down you make or lose $500.

Let's suppose that wheat keeps on going up and you sell out the whole ten contracts at $1.80 per bushel. What have you made (Illustration 5-1)?

4	contracts	— 20 cents profit	=	$4,000
3	contracts	— 12 cents profit	=	1,800
2	contracts	— 9 cents profit	=	900
1	contract	— 8 cents profit	=	400
				$7,100

Illustration 5-1

This gain was achieved on a margin deposit of $2,000 the original margin on four contracts of wheat. So you made 355 percent on your money, a goodly sum.

But now let's look at the market after you have made your last purchase of wheat at $1.72. Remember, every cent is now $500. What if the market goes down? Here are the figures (Illustration 5-2):

Margin deposit	$2,000
Profit at $1.72	3,100
	$5,100
3 cents decline to $1.69 at $500 a cent	−1,500
	$3,600
Maintenance margin — 10 x $350	3,500
Excess over maintenance	$ 100

Illustration 5-2

Thus, if the market declined another half-cent, you would be under the maintenance requirements and forced to either sell out part of your wheat or put up enough margin to bring it back to the $5,000 needed as margin on your ten contracts of wheat.

If you sold out, say four contracts at $1.69, you would then have the following situation (Illustration 5-3):

Total after 3 cents decline (see above)	$3,600
Maintenance margin — 6 x $350	2,100
Excess after sale of 4 contracts	$1,500

Illustration 5-3

Since the sale of 4 contracts leaves you with only 6, each cent of rise or fall is now only $300 to you so you know you will not go below maintenance unless the market declines over 5 cents from 1.69.

I have gone into pyramiding at some length because I want you to know that (a) it is a dangerous practice and (b) it is where many a large commodity fortune has been made in a short time. The odds against you doing so are fearfully high. You may be absolutely right on the eventual direction of the market but the small variations in daily prices almost invariably end up getting you where it hurts, as I have shown in my last illustration.

As the fellow said, "The way to make a small fortune pyramiding is to start with a large fortune!"

AVOIDING THE PROBLEMS
OF DISCRETIONARY ACCOUNTS

Occasionally, the speculator is asked to give some broker or some market service his discretionary account. In other words, you furnish the money and they will furnish the brains.

Presumably, they have better market savvy and better market information than you have so they can make more money for you than you can on your own.

While there are several successful discretionary pools based on using the medium and long term movements of the market, the discretionary account is sometimes a mere commission machine for the quick-turn broker. It can also be the vehicle much used by the broker who calls you by telephone from a thousand miles away and does not want all of his commissions eaten up by long distance phone calls.

I am against discretionary accounts and do not accept them. A broker knows that he can't win with a discretionary account. If it shows a profit, it is the customer's genius that somehow accumulated it; if the account shows a loss, it is the broker's fault.

Hesitate a long time before granting discretionary powers to anyone. It's your money and if you don't know enough about the game to handle it wisely, you don't belong in the game at all.

HOW TO TRANSLATE POINT CHANGES INTO DOLLARS

It is the mark of an amateur not to know how to convert point changes into dollars on any commodity in which he is trading. Your broker may remark to you wheat is up a cent and a half, expecting you to know what this is in dollars per contract. If you don't know how to do it, you're going to learn right now.

Amount of contract times point change equals value of point change.

Example 1. **Regular wheat contract = 5,000 bushels.**
Minimum price change of 1/4 cent − $0.0025
5,000 × $.0025 = $12.50 value of 1/4 cent change.

Example 2. Regular cocoa contract = 30,000 lbs.
Minimum price change 1/100 of a cent = $0.0001
30,000 x $.0001 = $3.00 value of 1/100 cent change.

Example 3. **Regular pork belly contract = 38,000 lbs.**
Minimum price change 2½/100 of a cent = $0.00025
38,000 × $.00025 = $9.50 value of 2½¢ change
or $3.80 per 1/100 cent.

Example 4. Regular sugar #11 contract = 112,000 lbs.
Minimum price change 1/100 of a cent = $0.0001
112,000 x $0.0001 = $11.20 value of 1/100 change.

Now you should have an idea of what your broker is talking about when he tells you cocoa is up nine points or sugar is down three points. Grains are usually quoted in cents and fractions of a cent. Thus, when you're told wheat is up a cent and a half, you know that it is up $50 plus half of fifty dollars or a total of $75 per contract.

If you are unfamiliar with the contract size and point change differential of any commodity in which you are interested, don't hesitate to ask your broker for this information. He will be glad to supply it.

Table 1. MAJOR NORTH AMERICAN COMMODITY EXCHANGES

EXCHANGE	TRADING IN
The Chicago Board of Trade	Wheat, Corn, Oats, Soybeans, Soybean Oil, Soybean Meal, Choice Steers, Silver, Iced Broilers, Plywood.
The Chicago Mercantile Exchange	Pork Bellies, Live Cattle, Live Hogs, Shell Eggs, Idaho Potatoes, Lumber, Milo.
Commodity Exchange, Inc. New York	Silver, Copper, Mercury.
New York Cocoa Exchange	Cocoa.
New York Coffee and Sugar Exchange	Sugar.
New York Cotton Exchange	Cotton.
The Wool Associates of the New York Cotton Exchange	Grease Wool.
The Citrus Associates of the New York Cotton Exchange	Frozen Orange Juice Concentrate.
New York Mercantile Exchange	Maine Potatoes, Platinum, Paladium, Plywood, Silver Coins.
Kansas City Board of Trade	Wheat.
Minneapolis Grain Exchange	Wheat, Rye, Oats, Flaxseed.
Winnipeg Grain Exchange	Oats, Rye, Rapeseed, Barley Flaxseed.

Table 1a. PRICE CHANGE DIFFERENTIALS IN MAJOR MARKETS

Commodity	Contract Size	Unit of Price Change per Contract	Exchange Minimum Price Change per Contract
Broilers	28,000 lbs.	1/100¢ = $2.80	2 ½ /100¢ = $ 7.00
Cattle (Live)	40,000 lbs.	1/100¢ = $4.00	2½/100¢ = $10.00
Cocoa	30,000 lbs.	1/100¢ = 3.00	1/100¢ = 3.00
Copper	25,000 lbs.	1/100¢ = 2.50	5/100¢ = 12.50

Table 1a. PRICE CHANGE DIFFERENTIALS IN MAJOR MARKETS *(Continued)*

Commodity	Contract Size	Unit of Price Change per contract	Exchange Minimum Price Change per Contract
Cotton #2	50,000 lbs.	1/100¢ = 5.00	1/100¢ = 5.00
Eggs (Shell Fresh)	22,500 doz.	1/100¢ = 2.25	2 ½ /100¢ = 11.25
Gold (IMM & COMEX)	100 troy oz.	1/100$ = 1.00	1/10$ = 10.00
Grains: Wheat, Corn, Oats, Soybeans	5,000 bu.	1/8¢ = 6.25	1/8¢ = 6.25
Hogs (Live)	30,000 lbs.	1/100¢ = 3.00	2½/100¢ = 7.50
Iced Broilers	25,000 lbs.	1/100¢ = 2.50	2½/100¢ = 6.25
Lumber May '72 contr.	100,000 bd.ft.	1¢ = 1.00	10¢ = 10.00
Orange Juice Conc.	15,000 lbs.	1/100¢ = 1.50	5/100¢ = 7.50
Platinum	50 ozs.	1¢ = .50	10¢ = 5.00
Plywood (CBT)	76,032 sq.ft.	1¢ = .76+	10¢ = 7.6032
Pork Bellies	38,000 lbs.	1/100¢ = 3.80	2½/100¢ = 9.50
Potatoes (Idaho)	50,000 lbs.	1/100¢ = 5.00	1/100¢ = 5.00
Potatoes (Maine)	50,000 lbs.	1/100¢ = 5.00	1/100¢ = 5.00
Silver (COMEX, CBT)	5,000 ozs.	1/100¢ = .50	10/100¢ = 5.00

In addition, GNMA Obligations are traded on the Chicago Board of Trade while Treasury Bill Futures and many foreign currencies are traded on the IMM (International Monetary Market, a division of The Chicago Mercantile Exchange).

Soybean Meal	100 tons	1¢ = 1.00	5¢ = 5.00
Soybean Oil	60,000 lbs.	1/100¢ = 6.00	1/100¢ = 6.00
Sugar (World)	112,000 lbs.	1/100¢ = 11.20	1/100¢ = 11.20
Wool (Grease)	6,000 lbs.	1/10¢ = 6.00	1/10¢ = 6.00

The above schedules are as of July 1, 1971
but are subject to change.

8

HOW TO SPECIFY ORDERS

Every once in awhile the average professional realizes very few of his customers really know about the routine of order handling and, more important, the different kinds of orders available to them.

Here is how an order is usually handled:

1. Your broker writes it up and hands it to his wire operator.

2. The wire operator punches it out on tape, rechecks it for any error and transmits it to the wire room in either New York or Chicago, depending on the location of the exchange.

3. That wire room phones it to the floor of the exchange.

4. The order clerk on the exchange writes it up and hands it to a runner who takes it to the floor trader in the pit.

You can see this process will usually take from one to five minutes. Add to this the fact the exchange tickers may be one to five minutes behind the market, you can see that often your executions may be at a different price than that showing on the tape when you put in the order.

Some firms are now in the process of converting this whole order procedure into automatic switching systems whereby the order will be sent directly from offices to the exchange floor, thus eliminating parts of steps #2 and #3, which should save time. However, this creates another bottleneck when there are more orders for an exchange than the computer can handle. You can speed up humans but the computer goes at its own pace.

So, let's return to the subject of your orders.

An order can be limited as to *time:*

1. A day order, good during today's session only.

2. A good through (date) order.

3. A good until cancelled order—called a G.T.C. or open order.

4. An "on the opening only" order.

5. An "on the close only" order.

6. A "fill or kill" order.

An order may or may not specify *price.*

1. A "market" order means to buy or sell at the market price prevailing in the pits when the order is received and executed by the pit broker.
2. A "limit" order means to buy or sell at the limit price specified or at a better price, if possible.
3. A "stop" order means that if the stop price specified is touched or exceeded, the stop order immediately becomes a market order and if filled at the best price obtainable. Some exchanges authorize the execution of a stop order on the bid or offer without a sale to activate the stop order.
4. A "Market if Touched" or M.I.T. order is the opposite of a stop order, although handled in exactly the same manner. If the M.I.T. price is touched or exceeded, the M.I.T. order automatically becomes a market order and is filled at the best price obtainable at the time.

Now, let's see how some of these orders work out:

Situation: You are long wheat at $1.50. The price is $ 1.45. You want to limit your loss, if possible, to $1.42.

Solution: You place a *G.T.C. stop order at $1.42.* Thus, when, and if, the market sells down to $1.42 your order will become a market order and will be sold immediately. If, however, the market closes at $1.43 and opens at $1.41 you would get $1.41, or so, on your $1.42 stop. The stop price is no guarantee that you will get that price. It simply is the price at which the market order provision becomes effective.

Situation: You are long wheat at $1.50. You think it may open much lower tomorrow. You are willing to take a two cent loss at $1.48 but if the price is lower, then you want to wait for a hoped-for price recovery.

Solution: You place a *day stop order at a $1.48 limit.* This means that at or below $1.48 your stop is activated but the order cannot be filled unless your wheat can be sold at $1.48 or higher during the day. Limit stop orders are often used by traders who do not want to get hurt by a fast move which they feel is only temporary. However, if you desire, you could also place the order at, say, *148 stop, limit 147½* which means the broker can not sell your wheat below 147½ but he has a little more price room to work in.

Situation: You are long wheat at $1.50 and the price is now $1.54. You feel wheat may hit $1.55 today and, if it does, you want to sell out immediately.

Solution: You place a *day order at $1.55 M.I.T.* That means the moment wheat sells at $1.55 today your order becomes a market order and the broker sells it immediately. He may get $1.55, though chances are he may get a little less. You, however, have now sold your contract at a profit.

Situation: You are playing a computer method which says to buy wheat if it closes over $1.55.

Solution: You place an order at *$1.55 1/8 stop on the close.* Thus, if wheat closes at $1.55 1/8 or higher your stop order will be filled at the closing price.

Situation: You have placed an order to buy wheat at $1.48. The market hits $1.48 but

Solution: Tell your broker to *buy at the market and on the same order to cancel your order at $1.48*. This way the floor broker will only have one order from you in his hands. If he fills the order at $1.48 before your market order and cancellation reaches him, he will send back the report at $1.48 with a note that the cancel was too late and he will ignore the market order that came with it. *But,* if you do not link your new order and the cancellation, the broker may get your market order before he gets the cancellation and, thus, fill both the $1.48 order and the market order. Always see that your broker links new orders with old if the market is near your price.

There are many variations of orders. I have merely tried to give you some examples. Watch yourself when giving an order to your broker. Remember, when you are short and you want to cover, *you buy-in,* you *don't sell out* your shorts. That's about the most common mistake and if your broker is not alert you may end up being short twice as much as before instead of being even up on your trade.

Some commodity exchanges will not take stop or M.I.T. orders. Others may take only stop limit orders. It is up to you to ascertain what restrictions an exchange has on orders.

9

HOW TO AVOID DELIVERY PROBLEMS

In the futures markets there always appears that time when the intangible suddenly becomes tangible; that Moment of Truth known as Delivery Time.

As you know, when you buy September eggs, you are in effect contracting to take delivery of that contract of eggs during September. This does not involve having somebody dump 21 thousand dozens of eggs per contract on your front lawn but it does involve your brokerage firm receiving a warehouse receipt showing that you now own enough eggs to make a week's omelets for the whole 101st Airborne Division. These are stored in the ABC warehouse and please remit the cash payment by tomorrow noon.

The brokerage firm will immediately notify the fall guy, you, and demand one of two things, (a) an order to sell your futures contract and to retender the warehouse receipt back to the clearing house or, (b) a check for the cash they will have to lay out for all those eggs—at present prices about $6,300.

Even if you have been foolish enough to get yourself into this mess, you may still be smart enough to tell your broker to "sell and retender." This means he will sell out your futures contract and at the same time give your warehouse receipt back to the clearing house so it can tender it to another sucker tomorrow.

Either way, it will cost you money since you will have to pay a minimum of a day's storage on your eggs, inspection fees, interest on the money the firm has had to put up to buy your eggs and, usually, additional commissions on your cash sale. You will also have the delightful chance of losing money on your cash eggs since they are tendered at one price and may be retendered at a different one. Also, eggs must be regraded before a subsequent tender so your eggs may not make grade the second time around. This is also true of hogs and cattle.

So, my *invariable* rule to all who want to risk delivery is:

Don't

Or, as a German forbear might have said:

"Nix, also *Nein!*"

Get out in plenty of time before your delivery date. Make a real point of finding out the earliest delivery day and get out before that day. Put your commitment forward if you still believe in it but:

Don't take delivery, ever!

Of course, if you are short, you don't have to worry about getting delivery. All you have to be concerned with is whether or not there is enough of the cash product around for the shorts to use for deliveries. If the supply is small, you may be caught in a short squeeze, a situation that sometimes make the gallows seem inviting.

There are some markets that make deliveries during the trading sessions and some which do not make deliveries until all trading in that future has ceased permanently. It is up to you to ascertain when your futures contract is subject to delivery.

Both the Chicago Board of Trade and the Chicago Mercantile Exchange make deliveries during the contract month. However, each has different rules and here they are:

The Chicago Board of Trade makes deliveries based on the oldest open net long position (Illustration 9-1).

| | Thousands of Bushels | | |
Firm	Net Long	Bot 10–19	Bot 10–2
A	30	30	
B	25		25
C	60		60
D	85	75	10
E	15		15

Illustration 9-1

On November 1, 40 M are received by the clearing house. Since firms B through E carry 10-2 as their oldest open date, the clearing house will allocate the deliveries as proportionately as possible. Firm B will get 10, Firm C will get 20 and Firms D and E will get 5 each.

You will remember this refers to net long position of the firm. If you are long, yet the brokerage firm you deal with is net short, you have no chance of getting delivery until its short position is eliminated. The only thing is that few firms will tell you how they stand, be it net long or net short on that particular delivery.

The Chicago Mercantile Exchange handles things differently and, if I may say so, in a manner more in the speculator's interest. Its method is strictly chronological. Each day it lists the nearest open long position on which delivery has been made and a total of the deliveries which have been made to date. If it has ten warehouse receipts to allocate, it takes the first ten oldest long positions in that delivery and hands the receipts to them.

Thus, if you are holding a long position bought in September and there were ten deliveries today on contracts bought between June 3 and June 10, you know you have little chance of getting a surprise delivery tomorrow and you, therefore, decide to hold your commitment at least one more day.

As I said before, some exchanges do not make deliveries while trading is taking place in that particular future. At the permanent end of all trading in that contract, there are left only a small number of professional long and short positions, people who want to tender or to receive delivery in the course of their normal business.

There is much to be said as to the pros and cons of having deliveries made while the future is still being traded. I remember the Chicago Mercantile Exchange experimented with having no deliveries made until all trading had permanently ended in each future. You didn't risk delivery but also you didn't know whether or not delivery could have been made if permitted and, thus, you could not gauge the comparative pressure of the cash market on the futures.

I believe the exchange tried it for awhile and then returned to its present system of chronological deliveries during and after trading sessions.

Most commodities are deliverable only during the contract month or a few days before its start. Sugar is the main exception and is deliverable about the middle of the month preceding the contract month and all trading ends on the last business day before the contract month.

Again, find out when your commodity is deliverable and get out a comfortable distance before that date.

10

THE ADVANTAGES OF CARRYING FORWARD

I have mentioned all commodities can be carried forward beyond the specified delivery date. This is how it is done.

Suppose you own December wheat futures in May. You have paid $1.60 per bushel for them and you want to get at least $2.00 per bushel when you sell your contract. However, late November comes around and, since you do not want to risk delivery in December and the price is only $1.80, you have run out of time on your December future. What do you do?

You sell out your December future on November 26 and buy an equal quantity of the May future at $1.90. If and when May gets to $2.10, you sell out and pocket a gross profit of 40 cents per bushel on your December and May futures combined. You have to pay two commissions, one on your December future and one on the May but you have accomplished your mission.

Why was May at $1.90 when December was only $1.80? Storage charges for five months. That wheat was harvested in July and stored in an elevator. Every month it stays there adds to its cost.

Carrying forward is used under many circumstances. If you have a loss on a May future, you can take your loss and buy September, hoping your loss will be cancelled or turned into a profit by the September future.

As you remember, right at the start of this book, I stated all commodities usually come back to a profitable price and the records bear me out. The process of carrying forward is a very necessary tool to use when proving that point.

Let's take an actual example:

The crop high of May 1965 wheat futures was set on June 3, 1964 at $1.63 1/4. Let's assume you bought at the high. At no time during the next eleven months did you have a chance to get out at a profit and you finally sold out on April 29, 1965 at $1.43 3/4 for a loss of 19 1/2 cents plus commissions of about 1/2 cent. Three days later, when March 1966 wheat came on the board, you bought it at $1.49 5/8. On December 14, 1965, March wheat sold at $1.73. If you had sold at that price, you would have had a gross profit of 3 7/8 cents, less 1 cent total commissions, on the two wheat transactions. If you had sold out when you got even, including commissions, you would have done so at $1.70 1/8.

But let's assume you are in this trade to make more money, you are not satisfied with either getting out even or making a 2 7/8 cents net profit. You want at least 10 cents for your trouble and money. Therefore, you do not sell out at $1.73 but hold until the last day but one of February, 1966 and sell out at $1.64 1/4. That gives you a profit of 14 5/8 cents less 1/2 cent commission or 14 1/8 cents against your previous loss of 20 cents. Your net loss is now 5 7/8 cents on the two transactions.

As soon as you sell out your March, you immediately buy an equal quantity of the December future at $1.64 1/4. Your objective is still a 10 cents overall profit which means you will need 5 7/8 cents plus 10 cents plus 1/2 cent commission or a price of $1.80 5/8 for your December wheat.

You attain this objective on June 15, 1966 and, thus, two years after you made your first commitment, you have finally realized a good profit from your investment.

What was this investment? You put up original margin of $500 per contract. This grew to about $1.500 (remember that 20 cents gross loss) during most of 1965, so let's say your average investment over the two years from June 1964 to June 1966 was about $1,000. Your net profit of $500 was 50 percent on your average margin so you made about 25 percent per year profit on your investment.

Yet, again and again, I must point out you need money to make money in commodities. Suppose you had only been able to put up your original margin? You would have lost it—or most of it—with no chance to get it back.

11

HOW TO USE OPENINGS, CLOSINGS
AND DAILY LIMITS

The trader soon learns that openings and closings on many of the commodity exchanges take place in a *range* of prices. This happens because with from twenty to four hundred men all buying and selling at the opening or on the close, there is bound to be a variation in the prices paid.

Therefore, each exchange shows those prices which occur during, say, the first thirty seconds and the last thirty seconds of each day's trading and records them as the opening range and the closing range of that day's prices. There are various time limits used by the exchanges, I have given only an example.

You will rarely see the opening ranges given in the newspapers and often they will also omit the closing range. So don't scream to your broker you have not gotten the price shown in the newspaper on your opening or closing order. Your order has been filled within the opening or closing range and that price may be a good deal different than the one shown in a newspaper.

I have never figured out who gets the good prices on these ranges. In my lifetime, I have been with four of the best brokerage houses and I don't ever remember having bought at the bottom price of a wide range or having sold at the top price. So, don't expect to get the best price in a range. You can count yourself lucky if you do.

Another fact you should know about openings is that some markets, notably most unregulated exchanges, plan their openings on a "call" basis. If, for instance, December, March and May silver are listed for trading, they will open December before the others. Once all the opening trading has been done in December, they will then shut that down and open March. This rotating call goes on until all the months have been called in order. When that is done, general trading in all months can begin.

This type of opening has the disadvantage that the first few deliveries usually have the widest swings, the traders are feeling for the proper price. Once they have determined it, the far months will have more sedate openings. Unless I am trying to take advantage of a wide swing opening, I usually will hold my order until general trading begins.

The call type of opening is a carryover from Europe where it is used extensively. Those exchanges with a comparatively few active traders use it so openings can be handled more efficiently than by general outcry at the start.

Another situation sometimes confronting the speculator is the "limit" day.

Each exchange has prescribed limits beyond which the price may not go during a trading day. These limits vary from commodity to commodity and are usually fairly wide. The limit is used for two reasons: the first is the protection of the brokerage houses and, the second, is to protect the traders. Where there is great excitement and action on any exchange the pricing machinery may get out of hand, there may be more buyers than sellers—buyers who will pay any price or sellers who will not trade until they have gotten their price.

In a situation like this, prices rise and rise and threaten to go out of sight. Here is where the daily limit feature steps in. Trades can be made at or below the limit price but not above it. If any buy orders are unfilled at the end of the trading day because of a lack of sellers, that is too bad and the buyer must wait until tomorrow's price before he can try to get an execution on his order.

Of course, there is nothing to prevent prices from opening up the limit or going up to it on the next day and even on several following days. In this case, the trader who is trying to get out of a bad situation may not be able to do so for several days and at a very bad price.

Then, too, many times prices do not hold at their limits during a day. They may hit the limit, then retreat, hit the limit again and close at or away from it. It all depends upon the state of the market.

On some exchanges, the limits are removed from the current delivery month. If, for instance, you are long or short September cocoa in September, the limit rule does not apply; the price is free to go wherever its pressures dictate.

Some traders who are caught in a limit situation, hedge their trades by using another delivery. If May pork bellies are up the limit but July are still selling a few points below the limit, they will buy July as a hedge against not being able to buy-in their May future.

Limit down days are just as frequent, some say more frequent, as limit up days but limit days, like moving day, are always tough. They would be a lot tougher without those limits, believe me!

I am listing the present daily limits on some commodities. These may be changed from time-to-time so don't take this list as gospel (Table 2).

Table 2. DAILY TRADING LIMITS

Commodity	Limit from Previous Close	Limit from High or Low Point of Day
Broilers	200 pts.	400 pts.
Cattle, Live	150 pts.	300 pts.
Cocoa	600 pts. A	600 pts. A
Copper	200 pts.A	400 pts. A
Corn	10¢	20¢
Cotton	200 pts. B	400 pts. B

Table 2. DAILY TRADING LIMITS (Continued)

Commodity	Limit from Previous Close	Limit from High or Low Point of Day
Eggs, Shell, Chicago	200 pts.	400 pts.
Hogs, Live	150 pts.	300 pts.
Oats (U.S.)	6 ¢	12¢
Orange Concentrate	300 pts. C	300 pts. C
Palladium	400 pts. D	800 pts. D
Platinum	1000 pts. D	1000 pts. D
Pork Bellies	200 pts.	400 pts.
Potatoes	50 pts. D,G	100 pts. E
Rye (Winnipeg)	10 ¢	20¢
Silver (Chicago)	1000 pts.	2000 pts.
Silver (N. Y.)	1000 pts. A	1000 pts. A
Soybeans	30¢	60¢
Soybean Meal	1000 pts.	2000 pts. A
Soybean Oil	100 pts.	200 pts. A
Sugar #11	50 pts. D	100 pts. D
Wheat	20¢	40¢

Notes: A—Limit removed on first notice day.
B—Limit removed on first day of delivery month.
C—Limit removed on eighth day of delivery month.
D—No limit on last trading day.
E—Maximum range becomes 100 points on first day of the delivery month.
F—Maximum range becomes 100 points on last trading day.
G—Limit becomes 50 points on first day of delivery month.
H—Limit becomes 50 points on last trading day.

These limits are subject to correction and adjustment at all times by the appropriate commodity exchange. I have tried to list them by points or cents rather than, say, $1 per lb. as a convenience to you.

12

HOW TO USE OPEN INTEREST
AS A TRADING GUIDE

Open interest in commodities is a measure of public participation in the futures market. It is created as follows:

A, B and C have no position in the market, then A buys a contract, B sells it short.
    One unit of open interest has been created.
A sells out his contract to C.
    No additional open interest has been created. C merely has assumed A's contract.
B buys back his short contract from C.
    This cancels *one* unit of open interest.

The mark of the rankest amateur is to say to anyone in the futures market, "There is a lot more buying today."

There may be a lot more buying but for every buyer there also has to be a seller. Open interest is the measure of whether that large amount of buying is really creating a greater public participation in the market or not. If it is, the open interest will rise. If the buying is mostly short covering by past sellers, then the open interest will not rise, in fact, it will drop since short contracts are being cancelled.

Do you see this? If not, take another look at the example I gave you at the start of this chapter. Open interest will rise if the public's buy orders are matched by *new* selling from professionals and hedgers. It will not rise, it may fall, if the public is not really buying but former short sellers are covering their short sales thus cancelling open interest, not creating it.

There, I've said it twice now. Let's not forget it.

Like many other facets of the commodity markets, open interest figures have their devotees—those who swear by and at them. Open interest totals of most commodities traded in the U.S, are published within 24 hours of their market appearance. Thus, the commodity speculator pretty well knows from day-to-day whether open interest is going up or down. And little good it usually does him.

As a generality in seasonal markets, open interest is usually building up during harvest. The reason for this is the producer wants to hedge to protect himself, as does the elevator operator who is buying the grain on a cash basis and hedging it in the futures market. Of course, if the public is greatly interested in the crop at any time you will almost invariably see a big open interest build up—usually with an eventual price collapse.

As a speculator, it would be well to watch open interest at all times but to take no action based on it *except* when it has built up to *three* times its average size for that same date during the last five years.

When this happens, it is usually near the top of a bull market which is about ready to collapse and well-margined short sales are in order. Some of the most spectacular profits I have seen have been started at such times.

Let's say you have the dates and figures shown in Illustration 12-1.

Year	Date	Open Interest ALL Contracts
1961	Nov. 10	200
1962	Nov. 9	325
1963	Nov. 10	175
1964	Nov. 8	500
1965	Nov. 9	350
Average		317
1966	Nov. 6	1000

Illustration 12-1

This is where the hard-boiled speculator gets interested. Any time the open interest is 3 to 3½ times normal, it shows large and usually foolish public participation in the market. Bullish talk is everywhere, everyone is buying. But are they? Remember, for every buyer there must be a seller and the fact that open interest is rising shows a lot of new contracts are being sold by hard-eyed men in the back rooms. Sooner or later the inevitable will happen, the market will collapse.

Now, this is not to say you will not have worries if you sell short when the market hits that 3 to 1 ratio of open interest. You probably will not sell at the top, often not 10 percent from the top, and you may have to endure several margin calls before the market turns your way. But eventually, almost invariably, it will do so.

I am showing a chart (Figure 1) of one of these 3:1 markets. It is a chart of sugar during June, 1967.

The 3:1 ratio was approached a little earlier, in May, and we started selling sugar at 2.90 for October delivery. Then, the Six Day War began and sugar rose practically overnight to 3.60.

At this point, many who had taken short positions in May panicked and got out with heavy losses. The rest, noting that the ratio was even better than before, put up more margin and hoped.

Their hopes were answered, as you can see. In less than three weeks, profits of 100 points from the highest price were available and in five weeks over 175 points from

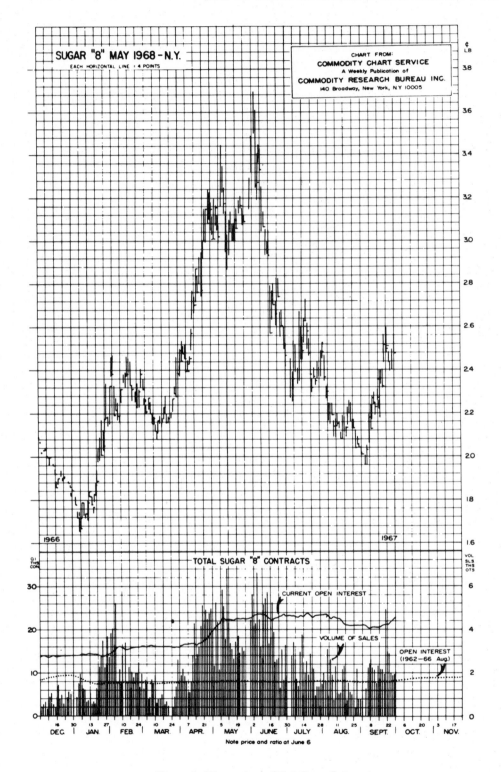

Figure 1. Illustration of 3:1 Open Interest

that high. As a matter of cold fact, we covered most of our 2.90 shorts at about 2.50 for a 40 point profit, although several rode it down even farther.

I have used this as an example since it shows that even though you may be on the right side of the market, you can also be temporarily wrong and you *must* have the money to see you through.

A natural question presents itself just here. Could the total of the open interest ever exceed the total of the actual crop? Certainly, it could since there is nothing to prevent avid speculators from buying as many contracts as their money resources will permit but as a practical matter, I doubt if it has ever occurred.

Many times, however, the open interest has exceeded the amount available for delivery in a specified commodity future. When this happens, you have the ingredients for a "short squeeze" with frantic speculators trying to buy-in their previous short sales at ever rising prices.

So keep a weather eye on open interest. Sharp build-ups or sharp drops may mean important money is getting in or out of the market and it behooves you to stay on the side that has the money.

Conversely, stay out of those markets which have only a small open interest. Lack of open interest means a lack of market depth so that you may have a difficult time getting proper prices when you get in or out of such markets.

13

PROFITING FROM SEASONAL MARKETS

Seasonal commodities are those which are harvested only once a year and are used during the subsequent twelve months or afterwards. These seasonals include all grains, cotton, cocoa and orange juice.

Pork bellies, hogs, cattle and eggs are not seasonals but are cyclicals. World sugar and all the metals are neither seasonal nor cyclical.

Rough rule of thumb states that seasonals are usually at their lowest price just after harvest and at their highest price two to six months after harvest. Thus the speculator wishing to profit from the price movement of seasonals will try to trade them with those considerations in mind.

These seasonal price movements also work to the advantage of the producer who wants to hedge his crop at a better price than he can obtain at harvest time when everyone is selling. This type of operation is known as *hedging* and is widely used by the producer, elevator man, the miller and others in the industry. I discuss hedging in another chapter.

However, seasonals sometimes do not work. In 1966, for instance, wheat was near its highest price of the crop at harvest time due to our enormous exports to that perennial begger, India. Thus, the trader who assumed the price on July 1 was going to be the low from then on had an expensive awakening. In 1967 and 1968, the very large crops made the seasonal a losing trade. However, the wheat seasonal returned to form in 1969 and 1970, scoring good gains in both years.

Let us look at the record on this wheat seasonal. As we have said, wheat is usually low at harvest and at its best price in December or March. Thus, we should buy wheat on July 1 and sell it out on December 1. Here are the results for the past ten years buying the first trading day in July and selling out the first trading day of December, using the March delivery (Illustration 13-1):

1961	2 3/8¢ profit	1966	8 1/8¢ loss
1962	11 1/8¢ loss	1967	14¢ loss
1963	20 7/8¢ profit	1968	9 5/8¢ loss
1964	1/4¢ loss	1969	5 5/8¢ profit
1965	13 7/8¢ profit	1970	25 7/8¢ profit

Illustration 13-1

From this deduct commissions of about 1/2 cent per year.

This is certainly a spotty record, indeed, for the ten years there are only five profit years. So, we are faced with our first big decision as seasonal traders; how can we protect ourselves against those loss years?

One way commends itself to us. If, after July 31, March wheat makes a new crop low, we will immediately sell out our wheat. This occurred in 1962, 1964, 1967 and 1968 and resulted in the following price changes from July 1 (Illustration 13-2):

| 1962 | 2 1/8¢ loss | 1967 | 3 3/4¢ loss |
| 1964 | 2 7/8¢ loss | 1968 | 5 5/8¢ loss |

Illustration 13-2

This idea certainly cuts our losses down in those bad years. However, we try to find a guide that statistically will tell us not to go into those bad years at all.

Observation of the past ten years shows us if the price of wheat on July 1 is either too high or too low, this seasonal has a dubious chance of success. By July 1, the December delivery has had about six months of history so, at that time, we plot the current price against that history (Illustration 13-3).

Year	Prices to July 1 High	Low	Range	July 1 Price	% of Range
1961	209 1/2	194 1/2	15	202	50
1962	224 1/8	213 7/8	10 1/4	220 1/8	61
1963	200 1/4	186	14 1/4	193 3/8	51
1964	185	147 3/4	37 1/4	149 1/8	3
1965	153 3/4	144 1/4	9 1/2	148	39
1966	202 1/2	159 1/2	43	188 1/2	67
1967	194 3/4	161 1/2	33 1/4	159 1/2	0
1968	167	136 3/4	30 1/4	137	1
1969	143 7/8	133 3/8	10 1/2	134	6
1970	150 3/4	140 5/8	10 1/8	144 1/4	36

Illustration 13-3

Plotting these figures against our loss years of 1962, 1964, 1966, 1967 and 1968, we find that if wheat is too high or too low on July 1, the seasonal will probably not work out. The best situation is to have wheat between 30 and 51 percent of its range on July 1. Too high, as in 1962 and 1966 or too low, as in 1964, 1967 and 1968 are indicators of poor speculative appeal. Of course, the 1969 percentage would have thrown us off a profitable trade but this is just to prove that no method ever devised has a 100 percent chance of certainty.

Our future trades in the wheat seasonal now have two guide lines. First, to plot the performance of December wheat for the previous five months. Second, to sell out our

March wheat if, after July 31, it makes a new low for the crop. These rules are not absolute but they may save you from some large losses while costing a minimum of profits. You might also use them to sell the seasonal instead of buying it.

The next seasonal we come to is corn. The harvest of corn is in the fall and, therefore, based on our seasonal hypothesis, we should buy corn about December 1 and sell it out on June 30 of the next year. Using the July delivery, this would have been the approximate result during the previous years (Illustration 13-4):

1961-62	6 1/2¢ loss	1966-67	22 3/4¢ loss
1962-63	11 7/8¢ profit	1967-68	12 1/2¢ loss
1963-64	7/8¢ loss	1968-69	2 3/4¢ profit
1964-65	2 3/8¢ profit	1969-70	10 3/4¢ profit
1965-66	6 7/8¢ profit	1970-71	6 7/8¢ loss

Illustration 13-4

From this we deduct commissions of about 1/2 cent per year, now 5/8 cents.

This record is about the same as wheat, five profits, five losses. Again, we have several large loss years and we want to devise protection against these losses being too large. So, we state that if after February 28, July corn sells at a new low for the delivery, we will sell out immediately. This happened in 1961-62, 1966-67 and 1967-68, resulting in losses of 6 7/8 cents, 14 cents and 2 1/4 cents, respectively. This would have been quite an overall saving.

Since our wheat analysis based on the relative position of the market showed fairly consistent results, we will now proceed to make one up on corn. To do this, we will take the price of July corn on December 1 and see whether there is a discernible relationship between that price and the yearly range up to that date (Illustration 13-5).

Year	Price to Dec. 1 High	Low	Range Dec. 1	Dec 1 Price	% of Range
1961-62	127 1/4	118	9 1/4	118 1/4	3
1962-63	123 1/2	111 7/8	11 5/8	115 1/8	30
1963-64	131 1/2	117 1/4	14 1/4	124 5/8	52
1964-65	131 3/8	123 1/4	8 1/8	129 7/8	82
1965-66	127 5/8	122 1/2	5 1/8	126 5/8	81
1966-67	163 1/2	141	22 1/2	153	53
1967-68	130 5/8	122 1/8	8 1/2	124 1/4	25
1968-69	127 1/2	112 1/4	15 1/4	123 1/2	74
1969-70	132 1/4	124 3/4	7 1/2	127 1/4	33
1970-71	168	134 1/2	33 1/2	158 3/4	72

Illustration 13-5

Illustration 13-5 shows very little if any consistency. Our loss years give no clear indications that they will be different than our profit years. The only fairly good indication is the high percentages in 1964-65, 1965-66 and 1968-69, all profit years. Since these highs occur during the animal feeding winter season, it may be an indication that corn is in shorter supply than usual or that competitive feeds are too high priced. The blight scare may have influenced prices to rise prematurely in 1970-71.

You might use this table in connection with our loss take-out provision after February 28 as previously outlined.

Now, to interpolate, just a word here about taxes. As you can see, your corn profit, if you have one, has extended over more than six months so it is subject to the long term capital gains tax which is usually a good deal lower than the ordinary income tax. Your wheat profit is only over a period of five months so that *is* subject to ordinary income tax. Remember always, that if a loss is now short term, one of the most important rules a speculator learns is to *never* let a short term loss become long term. Take the loss while it is short term—six months or less from the date the trade was started. Of course, if it is a short sale, this rule does not apply since all short sales in commodities are short term no matter how long you hold the position.

But to get back to seasonals. There are also certain well defined times when supply and demand appear to create opportunities for profit.

Buy March wheat on October 1 and Sell it out on December 1.

The basis for this is after the harvest time marketing of wheat is past, it takes awhile for the large amount of grain bought at that time to be used up. Prices may have gone down a bit in August or September but, by now, they are sometimes on a plateau awaiting new buying by millers or exporters. This new buying appears to begin taking place in November so that by December 1, the price level has gone up in response to it (Illustration 13-6).

Year	Price Oct. 1	Price Dec. 1	Profit (Loss)
1961	207 7/8	209 1/8	1 1/4¢
1962	206 1/2	211 1/8	4 5/8¢
1963	209 1/4	217 1/4	8
1964	152 1/4	151 3/4	(1/2¢)
1965	164 1/2	164 7/8	3/8¢
1966	181	185 3/8	4 3/8¢
1967	159 1/4	150 3/8	(8 7/8¢)
1968	126 7/8	132 3/8	5 1/2¢
1969	137 3/4	143 3/4	6¢
1970	170 1/4	173 3/8	3 1/8¢

Illustration 13-6

From this deduct commissions of about 1/2 cent per year, 5/8 cent in 1970, and you can see that this has been a good trade overall.

The next seasonal to be examined is an odd one. When it works it makes a very substantial profit. When it doesn't, it is a dog (Illustration 13-7).

Buy May Soybeans on February 15 and Sell them out April 15.

1954	63 3/4¢ profit	1963	10 1/8¢ loss
1955	24¢ loss	1964	9 1/2¢ loss
1956	66¢ profit	1965	4 1/2¢ profit
1957	1 1/8¢ loss	1966	3 1/8¢ loss
1958	7¢ profit	1967	7/8¢ profit
1959	3 1/2¢ profit	1968	8 1/4¢ loss
1960	3/8¢ loss	1969	3 1/8¢ loss
1961	40 1/8¢ profit	1970	4 1/2¢ profit
1962	5 1/8¢ profit	1971	14 1/2¢ loss

Illustration 13-7

Again, commissions of approximately 1/2 cent per year should be deducted, 5/8 cent in 1970-71.

When we use this seasonal, we are only interested in duplicating or approaching the big profit years of 1954, 1956 and 1961. How are we to get in when these profits should be coming up and also avoid the seasonal at all other times?

A study I made some years ago shows how this might be accomplished. The products of soybeans are soybean oil and soybean meal. Flaxseed yields linseed oil and linseed meal. While linseed oil is not considered edible and, thus, not competitive with soybean oil, linseed meal is competitive with soybean meal as an animal food.

With this in mind, I made a statistical review of the prices of Winnipeg May flaxseed and Chicago May soybeans and ascertained the following: in every recent year, when there has been a major spring advance in soybean prices, it has been preceded by at least a 25 cents advance in May flaxseed prices between January 2 and February 15. If this did not occur, no large net advance in the price of May soybeans took place between February 15 and April 15 (Illustration 13-8).

Year	May Flaxseed 1-2 to 2-15	May Soybeans 2-15 to 4-15
1954	28 7/8 +	63 3/4 +
1955	7 3/8 −	24 −
1956	34 +	66 +
1957	24 7/8 −	1 1/8 −
1958	29 −	7 +
1959	12 1/4 −	3 1/2 +

Year	May Flaxseed 1-2 to 2-15	May Soybeans 2-15 to 4-15
1960	18 3/4 −	3/8 −
1961	27 +	40 1/8 +
1962	13 1/4 −	5 1/8 +
1963	6 7/8 +	10 1/8 −
1964	5 3/4 +	9 1/2 −
1965	4 1/2 +	4 1/2 +
1966	11 1/4 +	3 1/8 −
1967	1 7/8 +	7/8 +
1968	1 3/4 +	8 1/4 −
1969	1/8 +	3 1/8 −
1970	6 +	4 1/2 +
1971	7 +	14 1/2 −

Illustration 13-8

This comparison clearly shows that in 1954, 1956 and 1961 there were large advances in flaxseed prices *before* those in soybeans.

It should also be pointed out that in 1966 there was a substantial interim advance in flaxseed prices during the January 2 to February 15 period. This advance of 17 cents, at its extreme, was probably trying to foretell the later than usual advance of soybeans amounting to about 70 cents during the summer of 1966.

The same thing occurred in 1970. Flaxseed prices rose over 15 cents in January before finishing with a 6 cents gain for the period. Soybeans advanced well over 40 cents during that summer. So, it is well to check the highs and lows of the January 2 to February 15 period when you are making your decision on the flaxseed price forecast.

There is another type of seasonal. It is the crop scare seasonal wherein the speculator is directly trying to capitalize on the grower's misfortune. There are two glaring examples of this type of seasonal, potatoes and orange juice.

It seems that at least once every growing season there is a real potato crop scare. Early frost or blight or something else always seems about ready to ruin the Maine potato crop with an accompanying rise in futures prices. During the six years, 1965-70, if you had bought May Maine potatoes about September 1, you would have made a substantial profit during the next four months in four of those years. In 1968 and 1970, you would have lost money (Illustration 13-9).

Year	May Potatoes @ Sept. 1	May Potatoes Highest Price Reached Sept. 1 to Dec. 31
1965	2.68	3.60
1966	4.22	4.72

Year	May Potatoes @ Sept. 1	May Potatoes Highest Price Reached Sept. 1 to Dec. 31
1967	3.05	3.94
1968	4.17	4.36
1969	3.18	4.22
1970	3.97	4.15

Illustration 13-9

While the subsequent high in 1968 was greater than the Sept. 1 price, I doubt if you would have been agile enough to get out with any kind of a profit. The price was about 3.30 on December 31 so you would have probably had a loss that year and also in 1970 when the contract was selling at 3.16 on December 31. The other years would, however, have shown substantial profits as you can see.

Orange juice concentrate is the second of our "disaster" seasonals. There always seems to be a fall hurricane or the threat of one which might damage the Florida orange groves though such damage is often more fable than real. But since September and October *are* the usual hurricane months for that area, the speculator is rarely without at least one hurricane scare to push orange juice futures prices up above summer levels. If there isn't a hurricane, then there may be a freeze or the threat of one in November or later which can have an electrifying effect on the price of orange juice contracts (Illustration 13-10).

Season	March O.J. About Sept. 1.	March O.J. Subsequent High to Feb. 27.
1967-68	39.60¢	67.00¢
1968-69	43.70¢	70.00¢
1969-70	41.65¢	55.90¢
1970-71	40.45¢	47.65¢

Illustration 13-10

Orange juice is quoted in differentials equalling $1.50 per 1/100 cents so you can see some very substantial profits were available from this seasonal.

There are many other seasonals. Here are a few:

Rye is harvested around July.
Oats are harvested around July.
Soybean harvest is September to November.
Cotton usually harvested in September to October.
Cocoa main harvest mainly September-November.

We will next turn our attention to cyclicals.

14

PROFITING FROM CYCLICAL MARKETS

Cyclical commodities are those which are grown every day, used every day, sold every day. There are not very many of them. The ones traded in the futures markets are pork bellies, live cattle, live hogs, shell eggs, iced broiler chickens and choice steers. All of these have active markets and all but the last two are traded on the Chicago Mercantile Exchange. The broilers and steers are traded on the Chicago Board of Trade.

Before we talk about trading these commodities, let's say a few words about the Chicago Mercantile Exchange. Only a few years ago, the memberships on this exchange were worth about $3,000 each. Today, the price is close to twenty times that figure. This expansion has been due to the heavy trading in pork bellies and live cattle. Pork bellies, in case you did not know, are the raw material for your breakfast bacon.

Each commodity exchange has its own little peculiarities and one of the situations on the Chicago Mercantile Exchange is the occasional wide price range of its openings. Of course, when you have many traders all trying to get the best price possible on the opening gong, you are not going to be able to greatly control the range of prices so paid. I have always found it a good policy not to place a market order for execution on the opening on this or any other exchange if I have reason to believe that the opening is going to be a wild one. Wait a few minutes and let the market try to settle down before putting in your order unless, of course, you are trying to take advantage of the situation but are prepared for possible unpleasant consequences.

In subjecting cyclical commodities to this analysis, it should be remembered only eggs have a trading history farther back than 1964 in the futures markets. So we have to trace the price history of pork bellies on the basis of cash prices rather than futures prices before that date. Yet, even so, pork bellies are a good medium to start our analysis of cyclicals. They may scare you to death while you are waiting for your cyclical profit but this profit is usually obtainable.

The first thing to remember, and remember well, is that the hog cycle is two years up and two years down. This is not a growth cycle. The hog growth cycle is about nine months from gestation to slaughter. The two year cycle is the time it usually takes to go from comparative plenty to comparative scarcity of hogs. Please note that I said comparative. There are always a lot of hogs around but sometimes there are a good many more than at other times.

Now, turn to your chart headed "Hog Slaughter" (Figure 2). The line indicates the rise and fall of hog slaughter. The individual yearly slaughter is shown just below the chart line and the two year totals are shown in brackets. Note the rise and fall of those two year totals—it is just as regular as the breathing of Mother Nature herself. You will note the chart line changes direction at the start of October of each year. This is the beginning of each slaughter year for hogs.

Why does this two year cycle occur? It is directly linked to the number of brood sows the producer buys, breeds, sells and retains. This might be summarized as follows:

First Year of Declining Slaughter:
Prices are rising. Farmer keeps his brood sows and buys more.

Second Year of Declining Slaughter:
Prices hold at a high level. Farmer retains his good brood sows now augmented by last year's births.

First Year of Increasing Slaughter:
Prices start to decline as farmer markets all the hogs that his increased number of brood sows have produced. Farmer starts to cull his older, less productive sows.

Second Year of Increasing Slaughter:
Prices go down even further as farmer markets an even larger percentage of his brood sows since their piglets will evidently not fetch a profitable price if the sows are bred again, and so on.

Note that I have not touched on barrows (gelded males). It is evidently the purchase, retention or sale of the brood sows which cause the cycle. This is probably an over-simplification. It is enough to know this two year cycle has been around for quite awhile. Based on this, 1970-71 and 1971-72 will be the two years of increasing slaughter, starting October 1, 1970.

The experts can say all they want to about the big factory-type hog farms being on a different basis now and that the little fellow who made the cycle is disappearing. He may have gone but the cycle is still with us. If it has gone, why were there 10 million more hogs slaughtered in 1966-67 than there were in 1965-66? The hog year of 1966-67 was the first year of the rising slaughter cycle.

Let's see how this has affected hog prices. If they are to run true to our cycle, they should be low in periods of high slaughter and high during periods of diminished slaughter.

Look at the bar chart at the bottom of the Hog Slaughter chart representing the yearly average price paid in Chicago for cash hogs during each calendar year. You can see that with the sole exception of 1951 our price-slaughter cycle has held true. The acute phase of the Korean War was 1951 and hog prices rose that year although they soon leveled off in 1952 to $16 in August of that year. From then on, every period shows the same history: slaughter up two years, prices down; then slaughter down two years, prices up.

Knowing all this, have pork belly prices followed the cycle? They certainly have. Let's try an experiment. Let's buy August bellies on October 1 of each year which

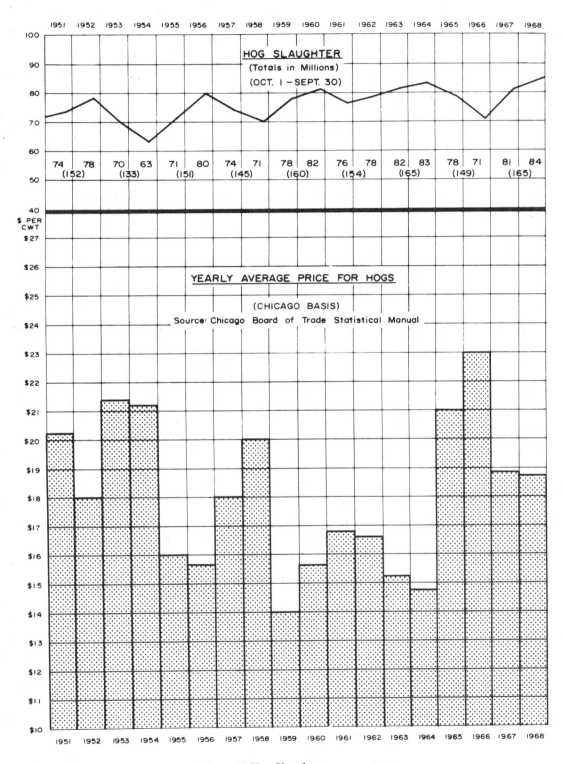

Figure 2. Hog Slaughter

promises to be a year of declining slaughter and sell them on October 1 of each year which promises to be one of increasing slaughter.

1966-67 First Year of Increasing Slaughter:
Price of August contract on October 1, 1966 was 35.60¢
Subsequent low to expiration of contract was 29.25¢

1967-68 Second Year of Increasing Slaughter:
Price of August contract on October 2, 1967 was 33.40¢
Subsequent low to expiration of contract was 24.22 1/2¢

1968-69 First Year of Declining Slaughter:
Price of August contract on October 1, 1968 was 32.80¢
Subsequent high to expiration of contract was 40.50¢

1969-70 Second Year of Declining Slaughter:
Price of August contract on October 1, 1969 was 39.60¢
Subsequent high to expiration of contract was 45.10¢

You can readily see that a 500 point profit (at $3 per point) was available in each of these years to the speculator who merely used our cyclical tool. In some years the prices went against the trend before straightening out but they always did work out to a profit of 500 points or more at some time during the trade. Since pork belly margins are usually about $1000 you can see that $1500 could have been made on the original margin, although some years additional margin was needed. These profits are figured at the old $3 per point rates.

The cycle also applies to the live hog market which is now an important trading medium on the Chicago Mercantile Exchange. However, the price history of this futures market is too brief to analyze.

Our next cyclical is shell eggs. The basic egg cycle is only six months. This is the time from a chick to a layer of medium sized eggs. Much can be made from this cycle.

Let us suppose that you and I are operating a big egg producing plant with many thousand layers busily working for us. The cost to us of each egg is about 23 cents per dozen. But futures on the Chicago market for delivery six months from now are selling at 40 cents per dozen. This works out to about 33 cents in our cash market. So, if the price would only hold up, we can put on five thousand more chicks and in six months they will be laying eggs. Eggs that we can sell at a good profit for 33 cents per dozen. But can we get that price? Everyone else may be selling a lot of eggs then and the price may collapse.

The answer is simple. We just calculate how many eggs we expect to have available for sale that month and sell the appropriate number of futures contracts at 40 cents. So, if the cash price in six months collapses to 25 cents, we sell our eggs for that but we also cover our futures contracts at, say 30 cents and make a 10 cents per dozen profit on them.

So, basically, if we are the egg producers who have sold futures against our production, we don't really worry about the cash price. If it goes down, the futures contract insures us against loss. If cash goes up, we lose on the futures contract but make it back on the cash price.

You can see that a smart producer can take advantage of this short six month cycle. So can the smart speculator.

However, (there is always a "however" isn't there?) you have to know some basic production facts before you start taking any position. The first and most important is to know how many chicks for egg production were hatched *last* year. These are the hens which will be laying the best this year. This total is known by February 28 each year and is published by the USDA.

Let's look at the previous figures for egg-type chickens (Illustration 14-1):

U. S. HATCHERY PRODUCTION (Number of Chicks Produced Commercially)
(Millions of layers)

Year	Number	% Change	Year	Number	% Change
1957	519		1964	528	3 +
1958	596	15 +	1965	488	8 −
1959	540	10 −	1966	569	17 +
1960	479	11 −	1967	534	6 −
1961	525	10 +	1968	514	4 −
1962	501	5 −	1969	529	3 +
1963	514	3 +	1970	567	7 +

Illustration 14-1

What exactly does this table tell us?

Look at the year 1958. That year 15 percent more chicks were produced than the year before, which foretells a lower price for 1959, the year these new chicks will be laying. What happened? Cash eggs in Chicago dropped from a high of 37 cents in January to a low of 24 1/2 cents in June.

Let's follow through on our analysis. The low price in 1959 discouraged a lot of producers so the number of new chicks hatched that year was 10 percent under the previous year. What should happen? Prices should go up in 1960. Did they? They did.

Cash prices rose from a low of 24 3/4 cents in February to a high of 55 cents in November.

But before you get too confident, let us look at 1961. Here, again, we are faced with a smaller hatch in 1960. Prices should go up in 1961, shouldn't they?

The high and low for January was 39 1/2 cents and 35 cents. The high and low for the year was 43 cents and 30 1/2 cents. It was really a "nothing" year when it should have been a bull bonanza. The fly in the ointment was that while hatch production had been below the previous year in the first part of 1960, it was above it in the last part, thus, foretelling no real up move in 1961. These hatch figures are released monthly so you can usually tell which way the wind is blowing.

However, let's skip down to the year 1969. Here, again, we have a situation where we have two straight years of lower production of layers. Should the price go up? It should. It did.

From the January low of 43 1/2 cents it soared to 63 cents by December in the Chicago cash market.

The futures market for December delivery reflected this by going from 36 1/4 cents in April to 65 1/4 cents in December. Had you held this contract your profit would have been about 29 cents times $180 per each cent, or over $5200 per contract if you had bought at the low and sold at the high.

You will have noted I have been quoting Chicago cash prices for my examples. I have done this rather than quoting futures prices since there are many delivery months in egg futures and these have a strong tendency to follow cash prices.

However, futures are what the speculator must trade in, so let's go back a few years to 1964 and see how we would have made out if we had bought or sold the September future on March 1 of each year (Illustration 14-2). By that time we know the hatch figure of the previous year so we can make a forecast of the price movement.

Year	Hatch Forecast	March 1 Buy	March 1 Sell	Interim Price Extreme	300 pt Profit?	Price Sept. 1
1964	Price down		33.00	32.00	No	35.30
1965	Price down		31.00	29.75	No	30.60
1966	Price up	35.25		43.90	Yes	43.60
1967	Price down		34.75	31.10	Yes	31.30
1968	Price up	38.20		41.70	Yes	41.45
1969	Price up	37.15		46.25	Yes	45.00
1970	Price down		38.00	33.50	Yes	44.90
1971	Price down		38.55	26.05	Yes	27.25

Illustration 14-2

This is a pretty good track record. Six profits, one break-even and one loss in eight years.

So much for the egg cyclical. Remember that six month period between chick and layer and don't speculate against the hatch figures. If the hatch says the price is going up, it will be foolish to go short the market. If the hatch is big, don't get caught in a long position. The consensus shown above tells the tale.

I just wish I could make up a cyclical for live cattle and choice steers but I can't. There is little or no agreement as to how long the cattle cycle lasts. Some say five years, others seven and some hold out for eleven years. Maybe you can figure out the length of this cyclical.

Iced broilers are the newest cyclical to have a futures trading market. The cycle from chick to broiler is roughly nine weeks so here we are dealing with a very fast changing market. From an analysis of cash broiler prices in the past, I would say the cycle is usually between 21 cents and 31 cents. Purchases near the bottom should be rewarding and short sales near the top would also seem indiciated. Remember, however, you should have at least three to four months before delivery when entering such trades.

Perhaps by our next edition we will have enough futures price history to enable us to make a real analysis of the iced broiler trade.

15

THE ADVANTAGES OF SPREADING

Spreading is the method of commodity speculation wherein you—

Buy one delivery month of a commodity *and*
Sell one delivery month of the same or another commodity.

Buying July wheat and selling March wheat against it is a spread. Buying July wheat and selling July corn against it is a spread. Buying May wheat and selling July corn against it is a spread. Spreads are usually put on simultaneously and should almost invariably be taken off simultaneously.

Spreading, or "straddling" as it is often called, is extensively used by the professionals in the commodity markets. They use spreads because they are trying to profit by a temporary imbalance in the prices of the commodities making up their spread. Such situations can be caused by many events: the seasonal tide of prices, excess supplies or the reverse, greater or lesser demand, crop news, weather, government programs and many other factors.

Now, how does a spreader make money? Suppose on July 15 you—

Bought May wheat at $1.50 *and* **Sold May corn at $1.25.**

On January 16 following, you liquidated·this spread by—

Selling May wheat at $1.65 *and* **Buying May corn at $1.30.**

You thus have a profit of 15 cents per bushel on wheat and a loss of 5 cents per bushel on corn or a net profit of 10 cents per bushel before commissions. The commissions would total about 1 1/4 cents so your real profit is about 8 3/4 cents per bushel. What would this be on a 5 M bushel spread? Remember how we figure point changes into dollars? Point change x size of contract = dollars of profit or loss.

In this case on the wheat side of the spread: 15 x 5,000 = 75000. Since 15 cents is 0.15 of a dollar, the decimal point should be in front of the 15 so that the correct equation is $0.15 x 5,000 = $750. This is your wheat profit before commissons (these total $30) so your net profit on the wheat side is $720.

Now, let's do the corn side. $0.05 x 5,000 = $250 which is the amount you lost on the corn part of your trade. To this must also be added commissions of $30 so your total loss on the corn trade was $280. Deduct this from your wheat profit of $720 and you have a net profit on the spread of $440.

There are several additional advantages to a profitable spread. You generally have to put a margin up only on the highest side of your spread. If the margin is $500 on wheat and $400 on corn, you will probably only have to put up $500 to margin the whole spread at the start. Of course, if the spread goes against you, more margin may be required. In the spread just shown, your profit of $440 would have been almost 90 percent of your original margin of $500.

Another advantage that the spreader can sometimes get is a lower commission. This occurs only when the same commodity is being spread such as buying July wheat and selling September wheat and does not apply to all commodities. Your broker can tell you if your proposed spread will entail a commission break on the combined trade.

A third advantage to the spreader is if the buy side of the spread works out to a profit and is held longer than six months, he will be able to secure the usually lower capital gains tax on such profits. This does not apply to profits made on the sell side whether held seven months or seven minutes. *All short sales are taxable as normal income and do not receive the favored capital gains treatment.* This third advantage was used on the spread I outlined. We bought our wheat on July 15 and sold it on January 16, thus qualifying the buy side profit for long term capital gains tax treatment.

I have said many spreads are seasonal. From our knowledge of seasonals, we know that wheat is usually low in July and high in January while corn is usually high in July and low in January. Thus, the plan of a spread to take advantage of this seasonal price change would be to—

> July 15:   **Buy March wheat and Sell March corn.**
> Jan. 16:   **Sell March wheat and Buy March corn to liquidate the spread.**

If you have a profit on the buy side, you can wait one more day. If you have a loss on the buy side, liquidate the spread one day earlier.

Now, why March delivery? Why not December or May or July? Since the spread lasts beyond December, you can't use the December delivery and because July is a new crop month, it will not come on the board until well into August. You could use May but March is sometimes better.

Having determined what delivery month to use, the very next thing every careful trader does is to look up the past history of his proposed spread. I would advise an eight to ten year history as a means of judging the spread. Here, therefore, is a twelve year history of the March wheat-March corn spread (Illustration 15-1). These results are before commissions.

1959–60	7 7/8¢	profit	1963–64	28 1/8¢	profit
1960–61	19 3/8¢	profit	1964–65	10 3/4¢	loss
1961–62	17 3/8¢	profit	1965–66	10 7/8¢	profit
1962–63	17 7/8¢	loss	1966–67	28 3/8¢	loss

| 1967–68 | 4 1/4¢ | loss | 1969–70 | 16¢ | profit |
| 1968–69 | 7 5/8¢ | loss | 1970–71 | 3 1/8¢ | loss |

Illustration 15-1

A 50-50 performance, six profits in twelve years. Yet, how about those loss years? They were not happy ones by far. More study of the spread is called for and you, therefore, examine past quotations and decide the spread should be liquidated immediately if:

After July 31, March wheat sells below its previous crop low, or
After July 31, March corn sells above its previous crop high.

This event took place in the six loss years and, strangely enough, in 1965-66, a profit year. Had you liquidated the spread based on this simple rule, these would have been the approximate results (Illustration 15-2):

1962–63	1 1/4¢	loss	1966–67	9 3/8¢	loss
1964–65	3 1/8¢	loss	1967–68	5 3/8¢	profit
1956–66	18 5/8¢	profit	1968–69	3/8¢	loss
			1970–71	1 3/4¢	loss

Illustration 15-2

These are all before commissions which used to total about 7/8 cents per spread and now are about 1 1/4 cents.

This points up a little known but very important fact. Getting out of a spread can be just as important as getting in. There is little point staying in a losing spread just out of stubbornness or plain hope. When you study your spread, check up on some method of getting out if it turns too much against you. It may save you a lot of money and heartache.

The veteran spreader is always looking for a "spot." Not just another spread but one that can truly be a source of profit this year. You show him the spread we have outlined and he says, "O.K., that's one. What else have you?"

Our next spread is a price spread based on seasonal changes to some extent but it is put on at different times of the year to take maximum advantage of whatever seasonal fluctuations there may be.

On July 1:   **Sell two contracts of May oats (10 M bu.)**
On Nov. 1:   **Buy one contract of May corn (5 M bu.)**
On Apr. 30:   **Liquidate both sides of the spread.**

The reason you equalize two contracts of oats with one of corn is oats are roughly one-half the price of corn but both corn and oats are used as animal feed. Again, we have a liquidating feature:

After February 28, if oats make a new crop high or corn makes a new crop low, the spread should be liquidated immediately.

Let's look at the performance of this spread during the last nine years (Illustration 15-3):

1961-62

July 1:	Sold 10 M May oats	78 1/2
Nov. 1:	Bought 5 M May corn	117 3/8
Apr. 30:	Bought 10 M May oats	68 7/8
	Sold 5 M May corn	115 1/4.

Illustration 15-3

Thus, we lost 2 1/8 cents on the corn and gained 9 5/8 cents x 2 or 19 1/4 cents on the oats for a profit of 17 1/8 cents before commissions. These then totaled about 1 1/8 cents.

Other year's results were as in Illustration 15-4.

1962–63	9 1/4¢	profit	
1963–64	25 1/2¢	profit	
1964–65	7/8¢	loss	Liquidated April 12
1965–66	12 1/8¢	profit	
1966–67	1/2¢	profit	Liquidated April 26
1967–68	6 1/4¢	loss	Liquidated March 1
1968–69	11 3/8¢	profit	
1969–70	7 1/8¢	profit	
1970–71	8 7/8¢	loss	

Illustration 15-4

Next, we come to the out-of-line spread. These are the spreads the professionals dream about, a price differential almost too good to be true. They occur but they don't last very long. You have to work quickly to take advantage of them, both in and out.

The first place I always look is the spread between Chicago wheat and Kansas City wheat. Normally, the same delivery month of wheat in these two cities does not sell at much more than a difference of 5 cents over or under. It should be remembered, however, while the deliverable wheat in Chicago is *soft red,* delivery of *hard red* will be accepted there at varying premiums or discounts. Hard red wheat is the Kansas City variety. Also, the freight and handling between Chicago and Kansas City is about 13 cents per bushel. Thus, when the price difference between Chicago and Kansas City widens to about 11 cents premium Chicago over Kansas City, one of two things will probably have happened: the markets are temporarily ignoring the facts stated above; or, the time to make delivery of hard red wheat to Chicago is too short. You can see that a wheat shipper located halfway between Chicago and Kansas City could probably ship in for 10 cents /bu. or less. However, it won't do him any good if he has sold short in Chicago and only has a few days to deliver in Chicago as the cars may not be obtainable or not get there in time or the warehouses may be full of somebody else's wheat.

All of which has been a preamble to the next spread. A typical example of the out-of-line spread.

On January 10, 1966, Chicago May wheat was selling at 11 cents over Kansas City May wheat. Many were alert to spot this big differential and, as it was only January, there was plenty of time for the spread to narrow. It did so and by April 28, Chicago and Kansas City May wheat were selling at the same price.

> **Jan. 10:   Bought K. C. May wheat at 159 3/8. Sold Chicago May wheat at 170 3/8 .**
> **April 28:   Sold K. C. May wheat at 159, Bought Chicago May wheat at 158 7/8.**
> **Profit 11 1/8 cents, Commissions 7/8 cents, Net profit 10 3/8 cents/bu.**

Can you tell me why we liquidated the spread on April 28 instead of May 1? Because we did not want to risk delivery of our Kansas City wheat to us.

I confess that I did not carry this spread all the way down to the wire. I liquidated it when I had 5 cents profit since this was approaching the normal difference between the two markets.

My justification for taking a normal profit was well rewarded in 1970. On February 18, 1970, this same spread was about 10 1/4 cents. Many spreads were placed around this price. By March 24, the spread had narrowed to about 5 1/2 cents, at which point many profits were taken. The spread subsequently widened again and closed on April 29 at 11 1/8 cents. It is well to take profits when "normal" differences are once again obtainable.

A more routine Kansas City-Chicago wheat spread is to:

> **Apr. 1:   Buy Kansas City September wheat. Sell Chicago September wheat.**
> **Aug. 15:   Liquidate the spread.**

This spread has had the history shown in Illustration 15-5.

1958	2 3/4¢	profit	1964	10 1/8¢	profit
1959	7 3/4¢	profit	1965	2 3/8¢	loss
1960	4 5/8¢	profit	1966	6 5/8¢	profit
1961	3 5/8¢	profit	1967	5 1/2¢	profit
1962	4 3/4¢	profit	1968	11 1/8¢	profit
1963	9 7/8¢	profit	1969	2 7/8¢	loss
			1970	4 1/8¢	loss

Illustration 15-5

Not a bad record at all, ten profits out of thirteen years. Commissions would have been about 7/8 cents round turn for the spread. Today they are about a little less than 1 1/8 cents.

Many of you are probably thinking: "Isn't there any other research we can do to determine the profit possibilities of a spread?" There is, of course, and sometimes it can be very helpful. Let's take the case of a seasonal spread which often shows a good profit but also, sometimes, shows a loss.

Aug. 31:   **Buy December Rye, Sell March corn.**
Oct. 31:   **Liquidate the spread.**

This has worked out as shown in Illustration 15-6.

1958	9 1/2¢ profit		1963	20 1/8¢	profit
1959	3 1/4¢ profit		1964	6 1/2¢	loss
1960	even		1965	2 3/4¢	profit
1961	17 1/4¢ profit		1966	1 7/8¢	loss
1962	1/8¢ loss		1967	1 1/2¢	profit

Illustration 15-6

I have deliberately omitted the years 1968 and 1969 until we make the calculations in Illustration 15-7. Since we are becoming a bit more expert in analyzing spreads, we note each loss year has been followed by a profit year, but we also are inquisitive. Could the size of the crop raised each year account for the performance of the spread?

Let's look at them; rye in millions of bushels, corn in billions (Illustration 15-7):

Year	Rye	Corn		Year	Rye	Corn
1957	28.5	3.0		1964	33.4	3.5
1958	33.1	3.3		1965	33.2	4.1
1959	23.0	3.8		1966	27.7	4.1
1960	33.0	3.9		1967	24.0	4.7
1961	27.4	3.6		1968		
1962	40.8	3.6		1969		
1963	29.2	4.0				

Illustration 15-7

Now, let's tabulate these results by years, ignoring 1/10 changes in corn and 2/10 changes in rye. If we are on the right track, these results should give us a pretty good idea of what to expect in future years from the spread (Illustration 15-8), based on the increase or decrease from the year before.

Year	Rye	Corn	Results	
1958	Increase	Increase	9 1/2¢	Profit
1959	Decrease	Increase	3 1/4¢	Profit
1960	Increase	Even		Even
1961	Decrease	Decrease	17 1/4¢	Profit

Year	Rye	Corn	Results	
1962	Increase	Even	1/8¢	Loss
1963	Decrease	Increase	20 1/8¢	Profit
1964	Increase	Decrease	6 1/2¢	Loss
1965	Even	Increase	2 3/4¢	Profit
1966	Decrease	Even	1 7/8¢	Loss
1967	Decrease	Increase	1 1/2¢	Profit

Illustration 15-8

Analysis of this table shows several interesting things. The most important, however, is in every year where the rye crop showed a decrease and the corn crop showed an increase the spread was a success. Also, this occurred in every year where the corn crop showed an increase and in every year but two when the rye crop showed a decrease.

By August 31 of every year you have a very good idea of the rye crop which has been harvested plus a government estimate of the corn crop so it should not be hard to get these figures.

Now, let's get back to the years 1968 and 1969.

For 1968, the rye crop showed a decrease but so did the corn crop. Based on the above analysis, I doubt if we would have gone into it, although those 1961 figures would probably have tempted us. The spread showed a 1/2 cent loss before commissions of about 7/8 cent.

For 1969, the rye crop showed an increase and so did the corn crop. Since every time the corn crop had shown an increase, the spread had been successful, we decided to plunge—and we were right. The profit for 1969 was 14 1/8 cents before commissions of about 7/8 cent.

The only fly in the ointment here is that rye is now only traded on the Winnipeg Grain Exchange. You can check back and see if Winnipeg runs on a price parallel to Chicago. It probably should but watch yourself when using Winnipeg, the markets there may be very thin. Use limit orders only.

I have given you this illustration solely to make you look beyond the raw price differentials of a spread and to find, if possible, the reason for the price action over the years. There is always a reason for price change. Try to find it before you place your orders, not afterwards.

Another technique you could use when researching your spread is to examine the prices reached before you place the spread.

Aug. 1:   **Buy December wheat and Sell January soybeans.**
Nov. 27:   **Liquidate the spread.**

1960	16 5/8¢	profit	1963	18 1/8¢	profit
1961	7 1/8¢	profit	1964	43 1/4¢	loss
1962	23 3/8¢	loss	1965	3 1/8¢	profit

1966	7¢	profit	
1967	10¢	loss	
1968	2 5/8¢	loss	

1969	7¢	profit
1970	5 3/4¢	profit

Illustration 15-9

In Illustration 15-9 we have a count of seven profits to four losses. The profits are nice but the losses can be horrible. How can we protect ourselves against the losses and still cash in on the profits? I suggest you might do it in the manner shown in Illustrations 15-9 and 15-10. Ascertain whether you are buying wheat near its crop low or selling beans near their crop high.

Did December wheat in July sell below its previous crop low?

Year	Result	Spread Successful?	This Indicator Correct?
1960	Yes	Yes	Yes
1961	No	Yes	No
1962	No	No	Yes
1963	Yes	Yes	Yes
1964	Yes	No	No
1965	No	Yes	No
1966	No	Yes	No
1967	Yes	No	No
1968	Yes	No	No
1969	Yes	Yes	Yes
1970	No	Yes	No

Illustration 15-10

Did January soybeans in July sell above their previous crop high?

Year	Result	Spread Successful?	This Indicator Correct?
1960	Yes	Yes	Yes
1961	No	Yes	No
1962	No	No	Yes
1963	Yes	Yes	Yes
1964	No	No	Yes
1965	No	Yes	No

Year	Result	Spread Successful?	This Indicator Correct?
1966	Yes	Yes	Yes
1967	No	No	Yes
1968	No	No	Yes
1969	Yes	Yes	Yes
1970	Yes	Yes	Yes

Illustration 15-11

One can readily see the performance of January soybeans (Illustration 15-11) during the past years foretold the future action of the spread more accurately than did the action of December wheat (Illustration 15-10). In nine out of the eleven measured years, it would have told you when to get in or stay out. You would have had four profits and no losses.

Another good way to use this tabulation would be to go in only if both "result" columns said "yes." This would have given you profits in 1960, 1963 and 1969 with no losses.

I did not evolve this or any of my other spread analysis ideas without a great deal of research as to what method seemed to work in the past. This is no guarantee that it will work in the future but it does give you a few road signs to observe along the way to your, I hope, profitable destination.

16

A PROGRAM FOR SPREADERS

I did not feel that I should encumber the chapter on spreading with too many examples of this type of speculation, since some of my readers would not be interested. The spreads in Illustration 16-1 are just some from a great file of them that I have gathered during my years of brokerage experience. I am not including any that I have already mentioned. The reader can interpolate these in the proper place chronologically if he desires.

The results shown are on the basis of the five calendar years, 1966-1970. Where the profits for the five years were double the total losses for the same period, I have marked the spread with an asterisk. All profits and losses were figured without allowing for commissions.

Before going into these or any other spread, I would suggest that the speculator attempt to research them and find out if there are any keys to their profitability as I demonstrated several times in the preceding chapter. There is almost always a key if you can find it. The search for it is usually more exciting than engaging in the spread itself. I hope you'll try to be a spread detective.

Date to Start	Spread Details	Date to Liquidate	1966–70 Years Successful	End of Spread Highest	
				Profit	Loss
1–3	Buy July Oats				
	and				
	Sell March Corn	2–23	4	1 3/8¢	4 7/8¢
2–8	Buy July Corn				
	and				
	Sell December Wheat	5–10	3	8 7/8¢	11 7/8¢
3–3	Buy October Flax—Winnipeg				
	and				
	Sell May Flax—Winnipeg	5–3	4*	14 7/8¢	14 5/8¢
3–24	Buy March Cocoa				
	and				

Date to Start	Spread Details	Date to Liquidate	1966-70 Years Successful	End of Spread Highest	
				Profit	Loss
	Sell September Cocoa	8—10	5*	139 pts.	——
4—27	Buy September Wheat—Mpls.				
	and				
	Sell March Wheat—Chi.	8—28	3*	11¢	7/8¢
6—1	Buy July Bean Meal				
	and				
	Sell December Bean Meal	6—28	4*	1065 pts.	315 pts.
6—15	Buy May Wheat				
	and				
	Sell September Wheat	8—1	3	2¢	3¢
7—27	Buy May Corn				
	and				
	Sell March Soybeans	9—8	1*	33 1/2¢	3¢
10—27	Buy March Corn				
	and				
	Sell December Rye—Winnipeg	12—8	4*	6 7/8¢	3 3/4¢
12—19	Buy July Copper				
	and				
	Sell December Copper	3—15	4*	125 pts.	50 pts.

*Gross profits for the 5 years at least double total losses for the same period.

Illustration 16-1

17

HOW TO USE CONVERSION AND SUBSTITUTION

A few years ago, I put a jar filled with yellowish balls on my desk. Out of curiosity, I would ask each of my customers to guess what those balls were. The guesses ranged from raw topazes(!) to chickpeas. Only about 10 percent gave the right answer which was soybeans. Here, many of them had been trading in soybeans for years but could not even recognize them in the raw.

Thinking back on that experience made me want to write this chapter. So much has been written and spoken concerning the relationship between soybeans and their products, meal and oil, and so much about the substitution of one commodity for another that I decided to put down a few guide lines of my own.

First, soybeans. You know soybeans have to be crushed into meal and oil. As a general rule a 60 lb. bushel of beans will yield about 11 lbs. of oil and about 47 lbs. of meal, the balance being waste. Thus, the governing factor in the price of beans should be the price that the crusher can get for the meal and oil.

This difference between the price he pays for his beans and what he gets for the meal and oil is known as his "processing margin," "conversion margin" or "crushing margin," take your choice. Bear in mind this is a gross margin, he must also add about 8 cents a bushel for the costs of running his crushing mill. This 8 cents figure is rarely achieved which is why there are so few independent soybean mills left. Most of the crushers are now owned by big corporations which rely less on the crushing margin for their profit than on an integrated operation which buys the beans, crushes them and sells them to the retail market in many forms ranging from margarine to animal feed to plastics.

It used to be that the production and consumption of soybeans doubled every five years. This rate has slowed somewhat only because the figures are now so large that doubling them is hardly possible in a five year period. However, the crop did increase from 845 million bushels in 1965 to 1,135 million in 1970, a five year rise of 34 percent.

One of the situations that has always titillated the speculator is the soybean "conversion spread." If the products are selling at a combined price below that of the beans, shouldn't this forecast a rise in the price of the products or a fall in that of beans? It would seem so since the crusher would be operating at a gross loss if the beans he bought were more expensive than the products he sold.

In the old days, when there were a lot of small crushers all over the soybean country this would have been true but these are not the old days and we have to evaluate the conversion spread in the modern context of the large integrated crusher already mentioned.

The mathematics of the situation are these:

> January soybeans are selling at $3.16 per bushel.
> January soybean oil is at 11.13¢ per lb.
> January soybean meal is at $78.20 per ton.

The yield from one bushel of soybeans is about 11 lbs. of oil and 47 lbs. of meal. These are the figures the Chicago Board of Trade uses in its manual.

$$11 \text{ lbs. x } 11.13¢ = \$1.22 \text{ of oil}$$
$$.0235 \text{ x } \$78.20 = \underline{1.84} \text{ of meal}$$
$$\overline{\$3.06} \text{ combined yield}$$
$$\underline{-3.16} \text{ price of beans}$$
$$\overline{(\$0.10)} \text{ negative crushing margin}$$

The crusher is not going to get rich at this rate! Either the price of beans must fall or the price of the combined products will have to rise for him to even approach a break-even point without considering his 15 cents per bushel crushing costs.

It would appear that under such circumstances an agile speculator could buy a contract of bean meal and one of oil and sell short a contract of beans and then just sit back and wait for the prices to adjust themselves in his favor. This spread (Illustration 17-1) known as a "reverse conversion" spread has a good deal of appeal at a time like this. (It is known as a reverse conversion spread because it is the reverse of what the crusher does when he buys beans to convert them into oil and meal.)

BUYING JANUARY OIL AND MEAL
AND SELLING JANUARY BEANS

Year	Spread @ July 1	Spread @ Dec. 31	Profit
1966	−11¢	+ 3/8¢	11 3/8¢
1967	− 5 5/8¢	− 5¢	5/8¢
1968	− 2 7/8¢	− 1 3/4¢	1 1/8¢
1969	+ 3/4¢	+45 5/8¢	44 7/8¢
1970	− 1 5/8¢	+24 1/8¢	25 3/4¢

Illustration 17-1

These are gross profits. Spread commissions which now total about 1 1/4 cents should be deducted so that two of the years show small net losses while the other three have very good profits.

But here is another compilation (Illustration 17-2):

BUYING JULY OIL AND MEAL
AND SELLING JULY BEANS

Year	Spread @ Jan. 2	Spread @ June 30	Profit
1966	−4 3/8¢	−12¢	(7 5/8¢)
1967	−2 5/8¢	− 2 5/8¢	0
1968	−2 1/8¢	+ 3 7/8¢	6¢
1969	−1 3/4¢	0	1 3/4¢
1970	+8 1/4¢	+10¢	1 3/4¢

Illustration 17-2

Deducting commissions of about 1 1/4 cents gives us two tiny profits, one 4 3/4 cents profit and one 8 7/8 cents loss.

This shows the necessity of picking the right time of the year to put on this spread. July appears a better time than January. The reason for this is that in July we are speculating on new crop possibilities (soybeans are harvested from September to November) and any new crop usually sells "plus hope." Hope is what makes the speculator's life interesting and it also makes for out-of-line prices. This is probably the reason why there were gross profits every year in the past five when the spread was put on in July and also why it had such an indifferent record when placed in January when almost all the hard facts of crop production and demand for the products are known and have been discounted. Such a market is selling "m.h." (minus hope).

Strictly speaking, the ratio of one contract of oil and meal against one contract of beans is not correct as to equivalents. Five thousand bushels of beans weigh 300,000 lbs. A contract of oil is for 60,000 lbs. and a contract of meal is 100 tons or 200,000 lbs., so the purist would insist on trading 10 contracts of beans (3,000,000 lbs.) against 9 contracts of oil (550,000 lbs.) and 12 contracts of meal (2,400,000 lbs.) in order to have approximately equal weights after crushing waste. But, the average speculator cannot afford such amounts so we will stick to our 1 *vs.* 1 + 1 analysis.

A question I am asked quite often is how do these conversion prices get so far out of line? Isn't it self-evident sooner or later the prices of the products will have to sell over the price of the beans? No, it isn't and, no, they don't.

The state of the market for the products is usually the governing factor. If there is too much meal, then there may not be enough oil. Again, the price of each may be too low or too high in relation to competing products such as corn vs. meal or cottonseed oil vs. soybean oil. Or, there may be an insistent demand for oil but none for meal which puts the crusher in a bind since, while he can readily sell his oil, his meal may spoil before he can sell it. Or, conversely, there may be a great demand for meal but he has no extra storage tanks for the oil that will result from the crush and, thus, can't take advantage of the big market for meal. Then, too, there is the matter of financing. He does not want to tie-up too much money in inventory even though he can get bank loans on a portion of it. So there are a lot of variables that the crusher and the speculator have to consider.

We have so far considered only the reverse conversion spread. There is nothing to stop the trader from putting on a regular conversion spread: buying beans and selling the oil and meal against them. But here you have the problem of how high is up? If the beans are selling 15 cents below the combined price of meal and oil and you feel this is historically too low a figure, what would be your profit objective? Should beans be selling only 5 cents below, 8 cents below or even? The crushing margin is 15 cents below so you may be putting on the spread at too high a difference when you do it at 15 cents below the combined price of oil and meal. The fact that this 15 cents figure is seldom seen in the futures markets buoys your spirits but you have that haunted feeling which says you may have gotten in at too high a difference.

That is why I prefer reverse conversion spreads. If I can put them on at a negative figure (the combined price of oil and meal totaling less than that of beans) then I know that I am not flying in the face of economics. I may be wrong but, by gosh, my idea was right! As to time, you should allot at least six months for this kind of a spread to work out. It may happen sooner, I hope it does.

Cottonseed oil is used along with soybean oil in the preparation of margarine and other foods but the futures market on cottonseed oil has almost vanished, so there is little point in discussing it. In the days when there was an active market in cottonseed oil futures, it was felt an actual price differential of 350 points, cottonseed oil above soybean oil, was a normal figure and any sizeable variation from this provided spreading opportunities. The 350 point differential was because the cottonseed oil was partially refined; whereas, soybean oil was the crude, unrefined product. I have put in these details in case the cottonseed oil market revives, as well it might.

I mentioned that some animal foods can and are substituted for others. In times of high prices, you always hear a lot about such substitution, especially when one commodity price is out of line with its competitors. If corn is high, there is talk that the producer can feed his animals wheat; if bean meal is high, then corn can be substituted. I have been hearing such talk for years and now will give you some items on these animal feeds in which there are active futures markets.

Corn is the basic ration of choice in the U.S. This applies to feed lot beef and hogs and to a lesser extent to broiler and layer chickens. Of course, many cattle are raised on grass and finished up to weight in the feed lots and some hogs rarely get anything to eat but scraps. However, with the growth of our industrial civilization, the raising and feeding of slaughter animals has become almost as standardized as the rules of baseball.

Wheat can be and is used as a partial substitute for corn when feeding beef and hogs but this substitution is usually limited to 50 percent of the corn ration at the most. Many feeders will not use wheat in this regard because it is a higher energy food and because the livestock find it unpalatable, although steam rolling and flaking help to overcome this complaint.

Oats can also be fed as a substitute for corn when feeding cattle but oats have the disadvantage of causing growth with little fattening. Therefore, the use of oats in feed lots is small. Oats are high in fiber and, thus, cannot make up more than 50 percent of a food ration for swine. Oats are also fed to dairy cows when such feeding is economical.

But oats represent a very popular item in the feeding program of replacement, egg-laying, poultry flocks because in this case the beneficial effect of oats are to delay the age of sexual maturity and the onset of egg production is also supressed due to the higher fiber content of the ration when oats are included in it. Thus, when the pullet flock is otherwise properly managed the result is for the initial, average egg size to be medium rather than small. Since the price of medium eggs is greater than for smaller sizes, one can see the benefit of including oats in the layers' diet.

Soybean meal is usually included in animal feed formulas because of its high protein content. While soybean meal may be only a small percentage of the ordinary fed animal ration, its overall use for this purpose is very large. Soybean meal forms a much greater percent of the total ration for laying and broiler chickens. The ratio here runs from two parts corn to one part 44 percent protein soybean meal all the way to four parts corn to one part 44 percent meal.

Milo, a grain sorghum, is also used extensively as an addition to or as a substitute for corn. However, there is little present activity in sorghum futures in the market on the Chicago Mercantile Exchange.

Alfalfa is the most important pasture and hay plant in the U.S. but there is no futures market in it.

The feeding of all livestock and poultry has progressed greatly in the last fifty years. Today's "critter" is fed a far more balanced diet than his owner. Vitamins, amino acids and various other additives are put in the feed so the finished animal will bring the very best price. Layer and broilers, too, have their own food regimens which are tested, revised and tested again so there will be more eggs per hen and larger breasts where, apart from Hollywood, breasts count the most.

With regard to these short notes on animal feeding, I recall a true story an associate told me. His father was a hog producer and had quite a number of them on feed. One day, he heard about the town brewery burning down. Out to the ruins, sped his father. He bought up all the beer in bottles, kegs and cans that had been salvaged from the fire. Sanitary regulations stated that the beer could not be sold for human consumption but what are regulations to a hog? So, for three weeks, my friend fed those hogs straight beer. He says that the hogs would lurch up to the trough, slurp in a stomachful of beer and then go over and lie in the shade with a look of almost human contentment on their jowls. This was living, kid, and they didn't like it a bit when the beer ran out and they had to go back to chopped corn.

This brings me to the *Corn-Hog Ratio.* This ratio is the market price of corn divided into the market price for hogs. Thus, if corn is selling at $1.15/bu. and hogs are $17.00/cwt., the ratio is a little less than 15. Interpreted, this means that for every dollar's worth of corn the producer feeds his hogs, he will realize a gross return of about $1.48 if the ratio remains constant.

This ratio used to bulk larger in the speculator's esteem than it does now. Government price supports and inflation have thrown it out of kilter. Today, the wise speculator uses it only if the ratio is 'way out of line with normal, which is supposed to be about 14.

Illustration 17-3 shows the ratio for the last ten years (July cash prices).

Year	Hogs/cwt.	Corn/bu.	Ratio
1961	$16.60	$1.14	14½
1962	17.30	1.10	16
1963	17.25	1.29	13½
1964	15.95	1.21	13
1965	23.20	1.30	18
1966	22.60	1.37	17
1967	21.10	1.29	16½
1968	20.30	1.11	18
1969	26.19	1.28	20½
1970	19.20	1.55	12½

Illustration 17-3

As I have indicated, I do not feel much use can be made of the corn-hog ratio by the profit minded speculator. The gradual rise in the index can probably be laid to the increased cost of raising hogs. These increases have been much greater than the per bushel rise in corn production costs. However, I would not like to be long hog or belly futures and short corn futures when the ratio is above 20 nor would I be happy being long corn futures and short hog or belly futures when the ratio is 11 or less.

Otherwise, in my opinion, using the corn-hog ratio as a speculative tool is far inferior to the cyclical methods described in another chapter.

18

HOW TO USE BAR CHARTING

Looking at the chapter heading gave me some amusement, I'd first written it, "Charting Bar-1" which made it sound like a ranch so I changed it around and now it looks as if I am running a slightly disreputable guide service. Which is as good an analogy as any to use when launching into a discussion of the "wheres and whys" of charting.

Let me say at the outset, the only reason for keeping charts is to *find and follow a trend.*

Every speculator is eternally searching for a trend which—when found or broken—can be ridden to a profit. In this ceaseless search for trends, charts have become a much used—and abused—tool.

Charts are like an ugly couple who think each other handsome; beauty is in the eye of the beholder. The same goes for chart reading. You may see something in them that I don't. While I am wondering if you have rocks in your head for not being able to see *this* formation; it's as plain as the nose on your face!

There are many, many books on chart reading and because these resources are available to you, I am going to stick to describing a few old patterns and give you a few new ideas. But please remember—remember always—charts are only useful to—

Find and Follow a Trend.

Most of the rest of charting is just like tinsel on the Christmas tree. It looks pretty but it doesn't help to hold the tree upright.

Turn to Figure 3. At the very head of the page you will see the basic bar marker showing one day's trading. In this case the highest price for the day was 150, the low was 149 and the close 149 1/2. The small horizontal bar at the right of the upright shows the location of the close. As a matter of simplicity, I will not use the closing bar in my illustrations unless needed.

When a series of day's trades are plotted one after another on graph paper, they often form patterns. These patterns vary in size, shape and length and often can be portents of future market action. Let's examine a few of these patterns:

The first is an "Upward Trend." This occurs when successive high points are higher and successive low points are also higher, as shown in the illustration of the Upward Trend. You will note I say the trend to be valid must have been in existence for at least

BASIC BAR ILLUSTRATION – – – – –

150

149½   Close

149

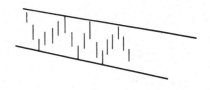

AN UPWARD TREND
Valid trends usually are at least two months

A DOWNWARD TREND
Valid trends usually are at least two months

A SIMPLE TRIANGLE
Market is coiling for a spring
Direction — ?

AN UPWARD SLANTING TRIANGLE
Market is trying to go through a top

A DOWNWARD SLANTING TRIANGLE
Market is trying to break thru
on the bottom side

A FLAG and A PENNANT
Indications of trend continuance, usually
Volume should diminish

A TREND IS BROKEN
Closing price must violate trend line

A HEAD AND SHOULDERS TOP
Basic formation for a reversal of trend

Figure 3. Bar Charting

two months. By this, I am talking about major trends. We will not waste our time on minor trends lasting a few days or weeks.

Our next pattern is a "Downward Trend." This occurs when successive highs are lower and successive lows are lower for a period of two months or more. This applies to a major trend.

When either of the above trends has occurred or is occurring, the chartist will draw lines touching the tips of the highest highs and lowest lows, thus creating a trend channel.

The channel is important to us. It defines the probable limits of any future movement within it. Any price movement going through its limits in an opposite direction to the major trend is a call for action. Thus, in an uptrend channel, a price movement below the bottom line of the channel would signify a probable change in trend. In a downtrend channel any price movement above the upper channel line would also be indicating a probable change in trend.

As a chartist, you will probably get into more arguments with yourself about the violation of channel lines than anything else. This is only human. If you are riding an uptrend with a good profit and the price gets below your bottom channel line, you should sell out but you don't. You think, "Oh, this is a false move; I've seen them before; I'll wait another day." Famous last words; the price the next day is usually lower than before!

As a rule of action, I would state here: *If the closing price violates a channel line in the opposite direction to the trend, get out of your position and switch to the other side of the market.*

Look at the illustration of "A Trend Is Broken." You can see the horizontal bar shows a close below the channel line. A get-out signal!

Of course, there are false moves where the price returns to the channel and the trend continues as if it had never been interrupted but there aren't very many of them in proportion to the times the trend is actually broken by a move through major channel lines.

As a practical matter, the breaking of a trend line is often more important to the trader than the trend itself. As I have said, it takes about two months for a major trend to show up and by the time you are aware of it, most of the profit has been drained out of the move. Therefore, having noted it, you wait for it to break so you can take the opposite side to the former trend. You will remember, I have said the seasoned spreader is always waiting for a "spot." So is the seasoned chartist and the breaking of a long trend is one of the easiest patterns to see.

Veteran chartists usually will not oppose a major trend unless it has had three separate stages. In an uptrend, there will be the first upthrust, then a period of consolidation, then a second upthrust and another period of consolidation and finally the third upward movement which often marks the culmination of the major move. This rule of three usually works better on bull markets than downward movements.

And remember, as a chartist, you have lots of company. There are literally thousands of people charting exactly the same movements you are. Thus, when a major move is signaled, you are liable to have a lot of the same orders as yours hitting the trading pits.

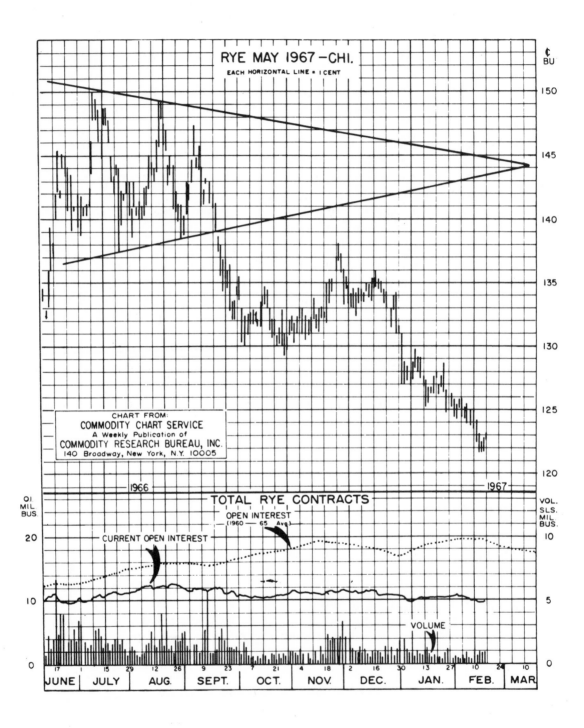

Figure 4. Simple Triangle

We now come to some of the other pretty patterns you will see on your charts. From now on, we are more than ever in the realm of the "occult." It's like the heavenly constellations. The individual stars form Orion or the Big Dipper from our viewpoint, but do the individual stars know or care that they are part of a pretty pattern? The same thing goes for chart patterns. They are there and we form them into shapes but is a price pattern real or is it merely a random assembly of prices which happen to form a pretty design?

I know you can get some very learned explanations why these formations are made but, frankly, I am not sure they have the significance usually attached to them.

The first pattern is the "Simple Triangle" (Figure 4).

This formation usually occurs when prices are tending more and more to a central level of equilibrium like a grandfather's clock that is running down. The closer the

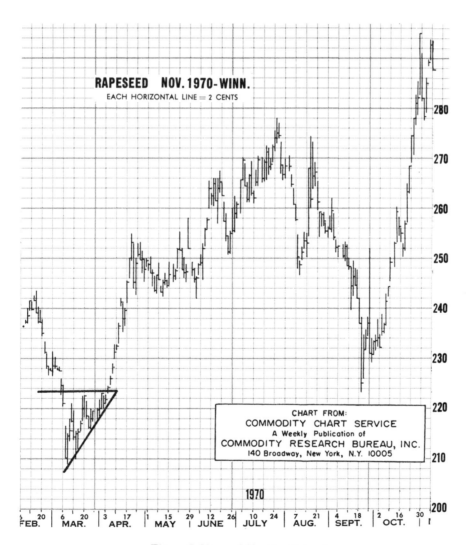

RAPESEED NOV. 1970-WINN.
EACH HORIZONTAL LINE = 2 CENTS

CHART FROM:
COMMODITY CHART SERVICE
A Weekly Publication of
COMMODITY RESEARCH BUREAU, INC.
140 Broadway, New York, N.Y. 10005

1970

Figure 5. Upward Slanting Triangle

daily price gets to the apex of the triangle, the less significance the triangle will have. A seemingly valid move will not violate either line farther along than I have put the "A" in Figure 3. A simple triangle in commodities will be anywhere from two weeks' to months' old. It can, of course, be a less acute angle than I have shown in the diagram.

The next pattern is the "Upward Slanting Triangle" (Figure 5).

This is usually found when the market is trying to go through a previous top. Time after time prices have banged against the same resistance level only to be thrown back. Again, the closer you get to the apex, the less reliable the movement is except that a close above the top channel line would be bullish. The bottom channel line must not be broken. If it is, it is a bearish signal.

Next, we have the "Downward Slanting Triangle" (Figure 6).

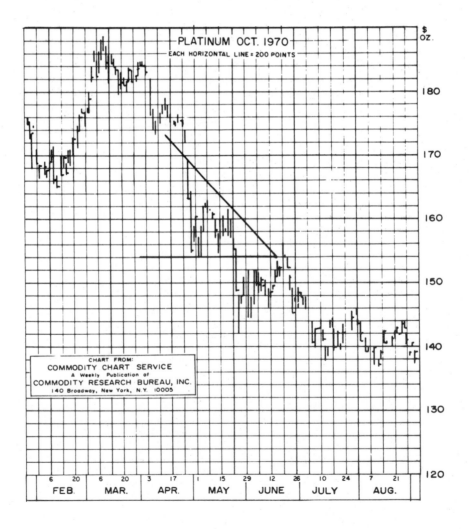

Figure 6. Downward Slanting Triangle

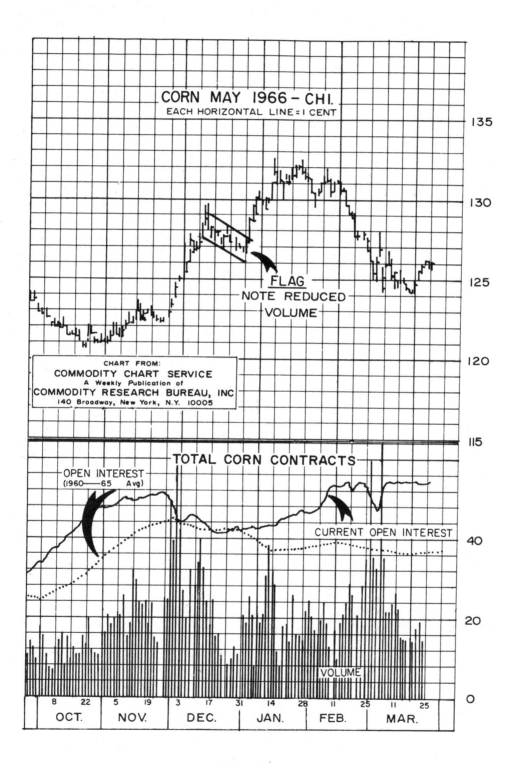

Figure 7. Flag

This is the very reverse of the Upward Slanting Triangle. Any close outside the triangle lines would generally be significant.

The "Flag" (Figure 7) can be very interesting formation.

During every move of any duration, there comes a time when profits are taken and the move simmers down while traders take stock of the situation. At this time, a flag or pennant is apt to form. These are formations which in case of the flag slant *against* the major trend and in the case of a pennant either against the trend or parallel to it. They are never too long in time, often only four or five days, but *they are almost always accompanied by a sharp reduction in volume.* Beware of the flag or pennant which

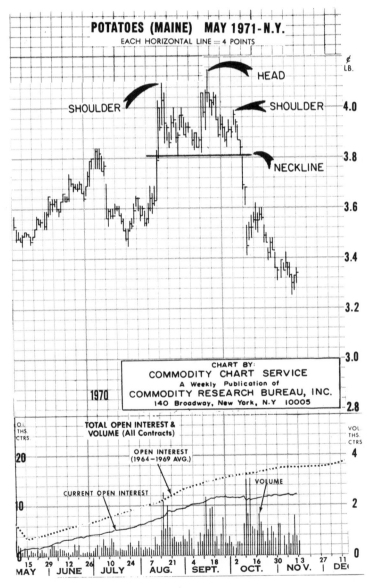

Figure 8. Head and Shoulders Top

does not have this reduced volume. You may be seeing a change in trend rather than a hesitation. After a real flag or pennant occurs, the market usually resumes its move. Some acute people say a flag or pennant usually occurs about halfway through a major trend.

One of the easiest seen and most reliable of chart indicators we come to next is the "Head and Shoulders Top" (Figure 8).

A head and shoulders is important because it generally indicates a major trend reversal. Here the market has thrust up, gone down a bit, then thrust still higher. Once again, it goes down a bit and then tries to thrust even higher than its last peak. If it fails to do so, there is too much selling pressure and it falls back to its starting place. You now can see the head and shoulders of the formation.

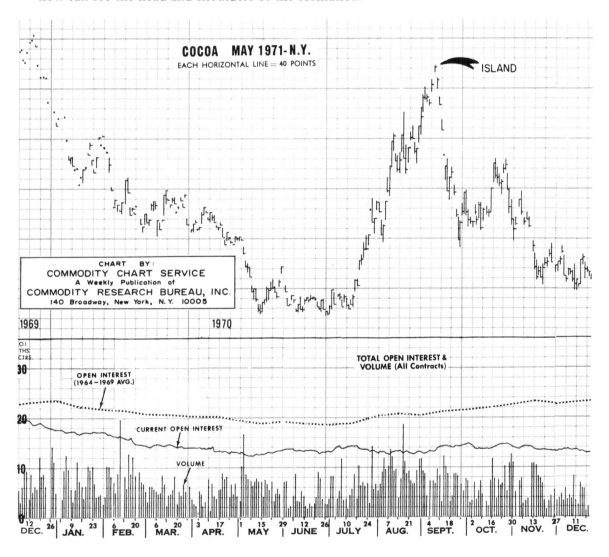

Figure 9. Island Reversal

The right shoulder usually is on smaller volume than occurred during the left shoulder and head formations. After the right shoulder has failed, the chartist will try to trace a neckline horizontally near the base of the head and shoulders and will sell if the closing price goes below the neckline.

Head and shoulders occur in both bull and bear markets. They are the basic reversal formation. If you do use them, buying or selling at a neckline penetration, as the case may be, be sure you have stop loss orders which will be executed if a subsequent close is beyond the tip of the head, thus indicating the formation was not a reversal after all.

A pattern chartists like to see is the "Island Reversal" (Figure 9). This formation is noted for being one of the more dependable forecasts of future price movements which are always *away* from the island in an opposite direction from the trend that created

Figure 10. Trend Lines

the island. Of course, if an island is neutralized by the right hand gap being filled a few days or weeks later then it is no longer a valid signal.

Figure 10 shows a major trend line. There are hundreds of other chart patterns; I have merely outlined some of the more important ones.

I have referred to volume several times but have not shown you how to record it. Volume is usually indicated by marks of appropriate length at the bottom of each day's chart (Figure 7). The lines will be vertical and the longer the line the greater the volume. It would be well to ascertain the normal volume on the commodity you are charting so your lines will not be too long or too short when indicating each day's volume total.

Some chartists also keep a dotted line near the base showing each day's total open interest (Figure 7). This may or may not be a valuable tool. To me it certainly is of little use about 99 percent of the time.

A final few words on charting.

Do not work your brains or your charts too hard. Wait for a real "spot" before you make your commitment. There are always dozens of trends forming or breaking in commodities so you don't have to be satisfied with a "maybe" situation; anyhow no more "maybe" than is anything else in charting.

Remember, you are charting to—

Find and Follow a Trend!

N. B. Probably the very best book on charting is a current copy of *Technical Analysis of Stock Trends* by Edwards and Magee. Your business bookstore is almost sure to have it.

19

HOW TO USE POINT AND FIGURE CHARTING

With the advent of point and figure methods, charting came of age—or at least to adolescence. It was a little like being graduated from Witchcraft I to Witchcraft II.

Point and figure meant that the chartist no longer had to make meaningless marks on a chart just because time had passed and every day a new mark had to be made like a prisoner checking off the calendar. Point and figure changed all that because it eliminated *time.*

Whoever discovered point and figure must have been an experienced speculator since he knew there was only one prime consideration in the market and that was *price.*

Where was *price* going? What direction? How far?

How far? There you have the real appeal of point and figure charting. How far? For the first time, the speculator could estimate the extent of a move, once it had started. If it had only this advantage, point and figure would be worth the cost of admission but it has other advantages too:

1. It deals solely with price and price change.
2. By charting only reversals, it gives a truer market picture.
3. It condenses much useless bar chart material.
4. It does away with many of the pitfalls of bar charting, "gaps" for one. There are many gaps in bar charting; break-away gaps, exhaustion gaps, plain gaps, all recognizable after the event but seldom soon enough to be useful.
5. About 95 percent of the exotic formations of bar charting are automatically eliminated. Triangles, diamonds, flags, islands and the like blend into the basic movement of the market and are not perceived to deceive.

Having said all this, I must put in a caveat. Almost all the successful chartists I know ("successful" means they haven't gone broke yet) use both bar charts *and* point and figure charts, using one to confirm(?) the other. So hang onto your bar charts, at least until the end of this chapter.

Here is how a point and figure chart is constructed.

For this method you will need a chart cross-hatched into a large number of equal squares.

Then, you must decide on a basic price change unit, not too big or too small. If we are charting grains, let's take one cent as our basic unit.

A day's price change has been: 147 1/4, 147 1/2, *148,* 148 1/2, *149,* 148 3/4, 149, 149 1/2, 149 3/4, *150,* 149 1/2.

The italicized prices are those which are one cent units which have differed by one cent from the previous one cent unit.

Your point and figure chart should record these prices thus:

```
150   X
149   X
148   X
```

The next day, we have the following full cent price changes: 151, 152, 151 and 150. These should be recorded as follows:

```
152   X
151   X X
150     X
```

This shows you the basis of the point and figure method. *When the trend reverses to a predetermined extent, in this instance one cent, this reversal is shown by a move to the next column.*

In this case, we filled in the squares for 151 and 152, then the price came back to 151. Our square for that price was already filled, so we had to move to the next column to find a blank square at 151. This movement to the next column signified a reversal of the trend.

Now, here is another sequence of prices. The first day, 149, 148, 147 and 146. Mark these on your chart. They make a neat vertical line. But here is tomorrow's opening price, 150. What to do? Moving over to the next column, you fill in the empty squares at 147, 148 and 149 to get to the 150 space which you also fill in:

```
150       X
149   X X
148   X X
147   X X
146   X
```

You can see that in order to get to the 150 square, we had to move to a new column since the 147, 148 and 149 spaces in the first column had already been filled by the previous trend. I said, you can see. Do you see?

A wrong way of doing this would have been:

```
150       X
149   X
148   X
```

```
                        147   X
                        146   X
```

Another wrong way would have been:

```
                        150   X
                        149   X
                        148   X
                        147   X
                        146   X
```

In both cases, you would be ignoring the fact the last figure in the downtrend had been 146 and you had to move over and mark all the intervening squares to 150 to indicate the uptrend.

There are *no* empty spaces in a point and figure vertical series. The only empty spaces in each column are those above and below the clumped, vertical sequence.

Still using our example, let's suppose the price now holds within the 150 area all the next day, not touching 149 or 151. The following day, it does the same. How do you show the activity of these two days on the chart? *You don't.*

This is one of the beauties of point and figure. You are not recording time, you are showing price change. If there is no unit price change, you make no marks on the chart, as if the two days of no price change never existed. If you have an inactive commodity, one or two *X*'s on the chart may represent a week's price change, whereas, on a bar chart, you would have filled out five horizontal spaces, willy-nilly.

I have gone to some lengths to explain the purely mechanical details of this method because even the most interested people find it a little hard to grasp at first. Once it is understood; however, there are no more mistakes.

Another thing you should do at the start is to substitute a 0 for an X every time the price ends in 0 and a 5 for an X every time the price ends in 5. When you have a great big chart all filled with *X*'s, it is easier to mark the *0*'s and *5*'s this way to orient yourself rather than to carry your eye back and forth to the printed figures at the edge of the chart. You should do it this way:

```
            151   X       X
            150   0 0     0
            149   X X X X
            148   X X X X
            147   X X X X
            146   X     X X
            145         5
```

This makes study of the chart much easier all around.

Now, we come to the first and most frequent objection to the point and figure method. You are supposed to mark each full cent price change during each day but unless you are in the board room watching a tape all the time, this is impossible. Can you reconstruct your point and figure chart from the figures in the daily paper? I would say, yes. You may lose a little veracity but I do not think it makes too much difference in the long run. Say, wheat closed at 169 last night. Today's range in the paper shows it opening at 169, high at 170, low at 169 and closing at 169 1/2. Your last X was in the 169 square so the only square you mark is 170. This represents today's recorded action.

The range the next day is opening at 170, high at 170 1/4, low at 167 and closing at 169. What do you do?

Since the first round cent after 170 is 169, you look at the square immediately below 170. It is filled, so you move over to the next column and mark 169, 168 and 167. But the market closed at 169. You look up at the 168 square. It is filled so you have to move over to the next column and mark the 168 and 169 squares. Your chart should now look like this:

```
170   0
169   X X X
168     X X
167     X
```

Any hands up? Good, we'll go on to the next problem.

A source of much discussion is what the reversal amount should be. In grains, some insist on one cent (as we have shown), others favor two, three and even four cent reversal charts. The same argument goes on in other commodities. Most chartists solve this by having two or three charts of the same commodity, a small (cent) reversal amount and, say, a three cent chart.

To my mind, you should have a chart or charts which most clearly tell you the tale of the market and which will most help your forecasting ability. Your chart is meant to be a road map on the path to Fortune. If it is too detailed or condensed to do this, then you might as well hang it on the wall next to Aunt Sophie's 1890 sampler which is also pretty and also useless.

Bases. Point and figure charting starts with bases. Unless a price series has been built on a strong base, there is very little you can do about interpreting its future action. There are a lot of different bases but let's examine a classic example (Figure 11):

The base in Figure 11 consists of a down thrust which forms the left side, the base itself usually with one or two upthrusts in the middle and finally a catapulted price up and away from the base.

How far is the catapult going to send the price? That is the real question. Point and figure chartists make a count across the base using that line having the most *X*'s but also counting the blanks between X's on that line to project the total amount of the catapult's strength. In this instance, it would be 15. This figure 15 added to the price of the commodity at the starting point of the flight would give the number of price change units that the price would be expected to advance from the base during the

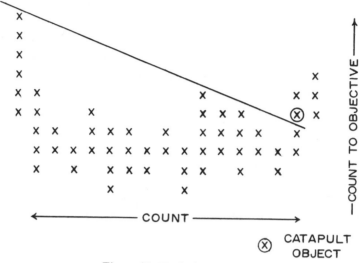

Figure 11. Typical Base

course of the move. This might take a day, a week or months but until a reversal base is formed against it or a change in trend indicated by other indicators, this count of 15 is considered the basic objective of the move.

It is this count which fascinates point and figure chartists. In any number of instances, the count has been exactly fulfilled. When it is not, which happens more often, the chartist actually feels cheated. He has watched the base form, seen the catapult, witnessed the price take off from the catapult and, then, instead of going from 150 to 160 as the count said it would, it gets to 155 and quits, going all the way back to 148. Mean, mean, mean!

A much less worse development is when the count is exceeded. The chartist buys at 150 with a count to 160. When the price hits 160, he sells out and is well satisfied—until the price keeps on going to 175.

There are many variations of the bases which are formed: fulcrum, compound fulcrum, delayed ending, head and shoulders and the like (Figure 12). There are also several ways of keeping the point and figure chart. As I said, some like to keep two or three point reversal charts, as a supplement to their usual one point reversal chart. In a three point reversal, you do not make any notations unless the move has gone three points in the opposite direction:

150	
149	X
148	X
147	X
146	X

The last price is 146, which is the low for this move. If the next day's price is 145, you would mark the 145 square as this is a continuation of the downward move now in

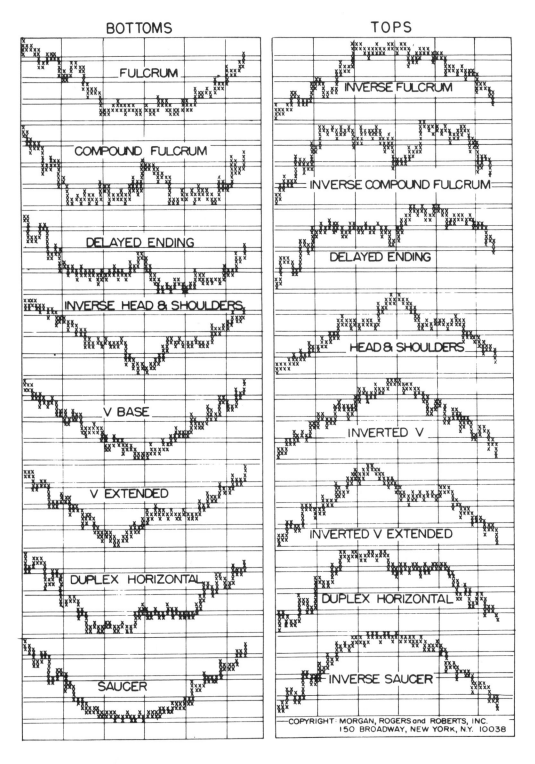

Figure 12. Bases

progress but if the next day's price is 148 high, 147 low, you would make no marks because to accomplish the 3 point reversal the price would have to go to 149. If it does this the following day, closing at a high of 149 1/2, you would mark the 147, 148 and 149 squares as an indication that the market had reversed the previous trend by 3 points or more.

The subsequent day the price is high at 150, low at 147 and closes at 147 1/2. What squares do you mark? The high at 150 continued the upward trend so you mark that square and, then, moving over to the next column, you mark the 149, 148 and 147 squares to indicate a 3 point or more reversal of the trend.

Two or three point reversal charts are necessarily more condensed than the one point variety. This is an asset when you are trying to spot a long term trend which may take a year to develop but the average commodity trader is not interested in such time spans. He wants to know what the present situation foretells and for this purpose a small unit chart is better.

Now look at the chart on May 1967 wheat (Figure 13). This is a one cent reversal chart, meaning, of course, that if the price changes from 190 to 191 or 190 to 189 an X is placed in the appropriate square.

The first thing you will notice is the upward trend line with low points at 178, 181, 191 and 195. This trend is broken at 198 and "Base A" begins to form. This works out to look like a "Delayed Ending" (See Figure 12) with two bases: A' and A," with a count of about 28 overall. Using a long fulcrum, you would probably buy at 193 with 193 + 29 = 222 as your major objective. A more realistic count across A" yields about 13 so you make 193 + 18 = 211 your first objective.

The market goes up to 202 and stops. Meanwhile, "Base B" is forming with a catapult object at 199. A count across the top of Base B yields a count of 11 squares so we deduct that figure from 199 to get an objective of 188. The market goes down to 191 and reverses itself, slowly forming upward "Base C."

This time the catapult object is at 197 with a count of 14 across the base for a total of 211. The price rallies to 208 and then begins to form downward "Base D." A sale is indicated at 203 with a count of 14 which gives an objective of 189. This is more than obtained in the subsequent move.

To recapitulate our trades using bases only:

A Base	Bought	193	Sold	199	6¢ profit
B Base	Sold	199	Bought	197	2¢ profit
C Base	Bought	197	Sold	203	6¢ profit
D Base	Sold	203	Bought	189	14¢ profit
					28¢ profit

I am guilty of only having skimmed the surface of point and figure trading. To do it justice, I would have to write a book about it and, since at least one has already been written, I refer you to its publishers noted below.

Please remember, however, point and figure charting, like its bar-type sister, is only useful to you to *Find and Follow a Trend.* There is so very much in charting that is

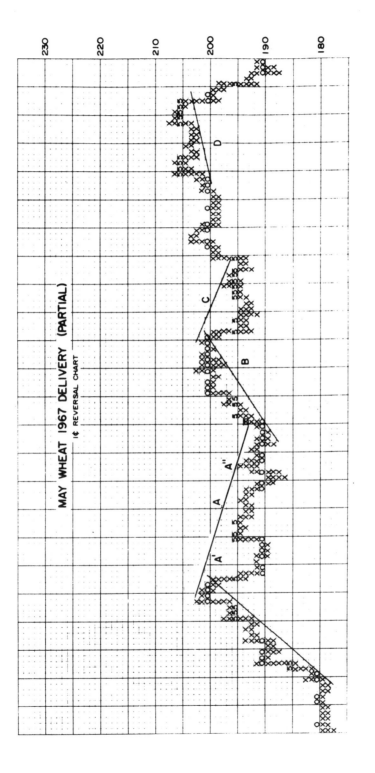

Figure 13. Point and Figure Chart

inconsequential and many, many formations that have no meaning. Don't try to read into a chart that which is not there and never has been there. Use it to *Find and Follow a Trend* or for decorative wallpaper, not both.

If you are interested in point and figure charting, I suggest you write to Morgan, Rogers and Roberts, Inc. The company publishes a book on the subject and also supply a plentitude of charts, guides, etc., all, of course, for a fee.

There is also a chapter on the subject in *A Guide to Commodity Price Forecasting* published by the Commodity Research Bureau.

Several other firms furnish daily, weekly and monthly point and figure charts which will release you from the labor of keeping your charts up-to-date. However, most chartists insist on keeping their own and I agree.

But remember, always remember, you are trying to—

Find and Follow a Trend.

20

HOW TO USE MECHANICAL METHODS OF TRADING

Mechanical methods of commodity trading usually use price and price alone to determine whether to buy, sell or hold. Because they do not require any decisions on the part of the trader, they have become more and more widely used by speculators of all kinds.

There are many types of mechanical methods. Charts, if they are followed religiously are one kind of mechanical method. Computer summaries—in which you are told what a mathematical formula thinks you should do—are another. Moving average methods are a third.

In all cases, you are still trying to do what I said was the basis of all chart analysis; you are trying to—

Find and Follow a Trend.

Don't get the idea mechanical methods are a product of post-World War II America. The late Ralph Ainsworth was investigating mechanical methods back in 1928 and some of the methods he wrote about went back to World War I. The only thing that has happened is the commodity markets are a lot bigger and a lot more numerous today than they were then and the number of speculators has increased manyfold.

But then, now and always, we are trying to—

Find and Follow a Trend.

One of the beauties of absolutely mechanical methods is they can be back-checked. You are dealing only with figures and these can always be traced back through the years, either on microfilm at your public library or through the yearbooks of the Chicago Board of Trade and the Chicago Mercantile Exchange. You also can keep your own daily file of the commodity section of *The Wall Street Journal* or your local paper. That is what I do.

The important thing to remember about any trend-following method is there are frequently long intervals when—to paraphrase Florian Slappey—" . . . the trend has suddenly become ain't."

When this happens, you are in a trading range market. You buy at the top of the range expecting a move beyond it. The market recedes from the high of the range and probes the lowest point. "Aha," you say, "that buy signal was false, the market is really going down." So you sell out your longs and go short—to have the market immediately turn around and head upwards again. This can and does happen two, three, four or five times in succession. By the time you are through with it and really sitting on the trend, you may have dissipated a full year's profits in a vain attempt to find a trend where there was none to be found.

I have used mechanical methods for a long time and I have yet to find one that is invariably successful year after year. Usually, the best methods will work three years out of four. The fourth year will either show a loss or a minor profit. The good years should show a profit of at least 100 percent on original margin so you can endure the bad year—that trading range year. But what if it comes first? It's liable to sour you on mechanical methods forevermore.

So, please remember no mechanical method is perfect; all methods will have their good and bad times and your only hope of an eventual solid profit performance over the years is to give any one of them a three year trial. Of course, you can follow several of them at the same time and thus shorten your overall trial times.

Mechanical Method for Pork Bellies

This is my favorite mechanical method. It has shown substantial profits in the years 1967, 1968 and 1969, a smaller one in 1970 and a fine profit in 1971.

Rules	Examples in the Price Tabulation
1. All calculations are based on a 10-day moving average of the closing prices of a nearby future.	
2. You *buy* if your last trade was a short sale or a false sell signal. You *buy* if the closing price has exceeded the moving average for 5 straight days *and* the market's price during one of those 5 days or subsequently has exceeded the previous day's moving average by 100 points or more.	See Jan. 13.
If, on the fifth day, the price exceeds the moving average of the previous day by 100 points, you buy immediately and do not wait for the close----------------------	See Apr. 6. (sell side)
If you have your 5 straight days above the moving average, but no 100 point penetration of the previous day's moving average, you wait until this occurs and buy at that time--	See Mar. 21.
All *buy* signals remain in effect until you have 5 straight days below the moving average *or* a 100 point penetration below the previous day's moving average on the down side. This negates all buy signals---------------------	See June 6.
Sell signals are handled in exactly the same manner except that you must have 5 straight days below the moving average *and* a 100 point penetration below the previous day's moving average during those 5 days or subsequent to them---	See Jan. 31.

Rules

If, on the fifth day, the price is below the moving average of the previous day by 100 points, you sell immediately and do not wait for the close----------------------

See Apr. 6.

If you have your 5 straight days below the moving average but no 100 point penetration below the previous day's moving average, you wait until this occurs and sell at that time--

See Oct. 19.

All sell signals remain in effect until you have 5 straight days above the moving average *or* a 100 point penetration above the previous day's moving average on the up side. This negates all sell signals----------------------------

See Apr. 24.

3. All commitments are for three contracts.

4. You place profit-taking orders 100, 200 and 300 points from your trade price--

See May 5, 8 and 9.

5. All outstanding positions are reversed when a reversal of trend is indicated by Rule 2. Thus, if you are still long one contract and get a valid sell signal, you sell 4 contracts, one long and three short sales--------------------------

See Jan. 31 for a complete reversal of position.

6. After the trade has been initiated, you place stop loss orders on all three contracts 200 points from your trade price---

See July 5.

7. After the first 100 point profit, you cancel the stop orders under Rule 6 and place stop orders on the two remaining contracts about 15 to 20 points on the profit side of your commitment price. This usually protects you against the market turning and going into a loss position while you are awaiting a valid reversal signal under Rule 2. You will find many trades are closed out under thus Rule 7---

See Mar. 29.

To illustrate all the above rules and the method, I am listing all closing prices and appropriate trades for the year 1967. Please bear in mind that this is a statistical study only and the trades shown were not necessarily made by me (Table 3).

Table 3. PORK BELLY METHOD TABULATION

March Delivery –– 1967

Date 1967		Close	Deduct	10 Day Mov. Av.	Days Above/Below	100 Pts.	Price Bought	Con-tracts	Price Sold	Rule	Pts. Profit (Loss)
Jan.	3	3470	3565	3523.6							
	4	3490	3535	3519.1							
	5	3495	3580	3510.6							

Table 3. **PORK BELLY METHOD TABULATION** *(Continued)*

March Delivery –– 1967

Date 1967		Close	Deduct	10 Day Mov.Av.	Days Above/Below	100 Pts.	Price Bought	Con-tracts	Price Sold	Rule	Pts. Profit (Loss)
	6	3485	3560	3503.1							
	9	3547	3597	3498.1	1						
	10	3500	3585	3489.6	2						
	11	3530	3477	3494.9	3						
	12	3570	3525	3499.4	4						
	13	3600	3472	3512.2	5	x	3600	3		2	
	16	3590	3435	3527.7							
	17	3632	3470	3543.9							
	18	3627	3490	3557.6							
	19	3610	3495	3569.1							
	20	3562	3485	3576.8	1						
	23	3632	3547	3585.3							
	24	3580	3500	3593.3	1						
	25	3600	3530	3600.3	2						
	26	3580	3570	3601.3	3						
	30	3515	3600	3592.8	4						
	31	3525	3590	3586.3	5	x		6	3492	2	(322)
Feb.	1	3575	3632	3580.6							
	2	3545	3627	3572.4							
	3	3527	3610	3564.1							
	6	3500	3562	3557.9							
	7	3520	3632	3546.7							
	8	3490	3580	3537.7							
	9	3495	3600	3527.2							
	10	3492	3580	3518.4							
	13	3507	3515	3517.6							
	14	3485	3525	3513.6							
	15	3435	3575	3499.6							
	16	3385	3545	3483.6			3392	1		4	100
	17	3375	3527	3468.4							
	20	3357	3500	3454.1							
	21	3370	3520	3434.1							

Date 1967		Close	Deduct	10 Day Mov.Av.	Days Above/Below	100 Pts.	Price Bought	Con-tracts	Price Sold	Rule	Pts. Profit (Loss)
	23	3382	3490	3428.3							
	24	3365	3495	3415.3							
	27	3322	3492	3398.3							
	28	3330	3507	3380.6							
Mar.	1	3430	3485	3375.1			3480	2		7	24

Loss to Date--- (198)

Table 3. PORK BELLY METHOD TABULATION (Continued)

May Delivery − − 1967

Date 1967		Close	Deduct	10 Day Mov.Av.	Days Above/Below	100 Pts.	Price Bought	Con-tracts	Price Sold	Rule	Pts. Profit (Loss)
Mar.	1	3500	3537	3440.8	1						
	2	3430	3532	3430.6							
	3	3422	3445	3428.3							
	6	3465	3435	3431.3	1						
	7	3450	3422	3434.1	2						
	8	3447	3437	3435.1	3						
	9	3475	3445	3438.1	4						
	10	3497	3425	3445.3	5						
	13	3472	3380	3454.5							
	14	3485	3387	3464.3							
	15	3495	3500	3463.8							
	16	3555	3430	3476.3							
	17	3547	3422	3488.8							
	20	3552	3465	3497.5							
	21	3610	3450	3513.5		x	3597	3		2	
	22	3680	3447	3536.8				1	3697	4	100
	23	3667	3475	3556.0							
	27	3650	3497	3571.3							
	28	3627	3472	3586.8							
	29	3660	3485	3604.3				2	3610	7	26
	30	3637	3495	3618.5							
	31	3600	3555	3623.0	1						

Table 3. PORK BELLY METHOD TABULATION (Continued)

May Delivery −− 1967

Date 1967		Close	Deduct	10 Day Mov.Av.	Days Above/Below	100 Pts.	Price Bought	Con-tracts	Price Sold	Rule	Pts. Profit (Loss)
Apr.	3	3575	3547	3625.8	2						
	4	3585	3552	3629.1	3						
	5	3552	3610	3623.3	4						
	6	3470	3680	3602.3	5	x		3	3522	2	
	7	3450	3667	3580.6							
	10	3427	3650	3558.3			3422	1		4	100
	11	3475	3627	3543.1							
	12	3410	3660	3518.1							
	13	3385	3637	3492.9							
	14	3405	3600	3473.4							
	17	3505	3575	3466.4			3510	2		7	24
	18	3450	3585	3452.7							
	19	3450	3552	3442.7							

Profit to Date-----52

Table 3. PORK BELLY METHOD TABULATION (Continued)

August Delivery − − 1967

Date 1967		Close	Deduct	10 Day Mov.Av.	Days Above/Below	100 Pts.	Price Bought	Con-tracts	Price Sold	Rule	Pts. Profit (Loss)
Apr.	19	3465	3560	3459.6	1						
	20	3477	3505	3456.8	2						
	21	3477	3512	3453.3	3						
	24	3555	3430	3465.8	4	x					
	25	3530	3470	3471.8	5		3530	3		2	
	26	3582	3437	3486.3							
	27	3462	3390	3503.5							
	28	3515	3415	3513.5							
May	1	3512	3512	3513.5	1						
	2	3542	3460	3521.7							
	3	3545	3465	3529.7							

Table 3. PORK BELLY METHOD TABULATION (Continued)
August Delivery –– 1967

Date 1967		Close	Deduct	10 Day Mov.Av.	Days Above/Below	100 Pts.	Price Bought	Con-tracts	Price Sold	Rule	Pts. Profit (Loss)
	4	3550	3477	3537.0							
	5	3642	3477	3553.5				1	3630	4	100
	8	3795	3555	3577.5				1	3730	4	200
	9	3840	3530	3608.5				1	3830	4	300
	10	3885	3582	3638.8							
	11	3820	3562	3664.6							
	12	3887	3515	3701.8							
	15	4025	3512	3753.1							
	16	4180	3542	3816.9							
	17	4100	3545	3872.4							
	18	4225	3550	3939.9							
	19	4195	3642	3995.2							
	22	4165	3795	4032.2							
	23	4290	3840	4077.2							
	24	4250	3885	4113.7							
	25	4215	3820	4153.2							
	26	4320	3887	4196.5							
	29	4247	4025	4218.7							
	31	4340	4180	4234.7							
June	1	4270	4100	4251.7							
	2	4197	4225	4248.9	1						
	5	4200	4195	4249.4	2						
	6	4115	4165	4244.4	3	x					
	7	3982	4290	4213.6	4						
	8	4055	4250	4194.1	5			3	4055	2	
	9	3945	4215	4167.1			3955	1		4	100
	12	4037	4320	4138.8							
	13	3882	4247	4102.3							
	14	3832	4340	4051.5			3855	1		4	200
	15	3802	4270	4004.7							
	16	3915	4197	3976.5							
	19	3835	4200	3940.0							
	20	3815	4115	3910.0			3755	1		4	300

Table 3. PORK BELLY METHOD TABULATION (Continued)

August Delivery — — 1967

Date 1967	Close	Deduct	10 Day Mov.Av.	Days Above/Below	100 Pts.	Price Bought	Con- tracts	Price Sold	Rule	Pts. Profit (Loss)
21	3835	3982	3895.3							
22	3975	4055	3887.3	1						
23	3955	3945	3888.3	2						
26	4060	4037	3890.6	3	x					
27	4112	3882	3913.6	4						
28	4010	3832	3931.4	5		4010	3		2	
29	4020	3802	3953.2							
30	3955	3915	3957.2	1						

Profit to Date---------- 1252

Table 3. PORK BELLY TABULATION (Continued)

August Delivery — — 1967

Date 1967	Close	Deduct	10 Day Mov.Av.	Days Above/Below	100 Pts.	Price Bought	Con- tracts	Price Sold	Rule	Pts. Profit (Loss)
July 3	3895	3835	3963.2	2						
5	3780	3815	3959.7	3	x		3	3810	6	(600)
6	3835	3835	3959.7	4						
7	3712	3975	3933.4	5			3	3712	2	
10	3555	3955	3893.4			3612	1		4	100
11	3600	4060	3847.4			3512	1		4	200
12	3447	4112	3780.9							
13	3302	4010	3710.1			3412	1		4	300
14	3330	4020	3641.1							
17	3290	3955	3574.6							
18	3165	3895	3501.6							
19	3260	3780	3449.6							
20	3397	3835	3405.8							
21	3370	3712	3371.6							
24	3215	3555	3337.6							
25	3065	3600	3284.1							

Table 3. PORK BELLY TABULATION (Continued)

August Delivery — — 1967

Date 1967		Close	Deduct	10 Day Mov.Av.	Days Above/Below	100 Pts.	Price Bought	Con-tracts	Price Sold	Rule	Pts. Profit (Loss)
	26	3095	3447	3248.9							
	27	3175	3302	3236.2							
	28	3170	3330	3220.2							
	31	3255	3290	3216.7	1						
Aug.	1	3107	3165	3210.9							
	2	3180	3260.	3202.9							
	3	3150	3397	3178.0							
	4	3230	3370	3164.0	1	x					——

Profits to Date------ 1252

Table 3. PORK BELLY METHOD TABULATION

February Delivery — — 1968

Date 1967		Close	Deduct	10 Day Mov.Av.	Days Above/Below	100 Pts.	Price Bought	Con-tracts	Price Sold	Rule	Pts. Profit (Loss)
Aug.	4	3452	3617	3421.2	1						
	7	3432	3475	3416.9	2						
	8	3420	3325	3426.4							
	9	3387	3400	3425.1							
	10	3335	3485	3410.1							
	11	3360	3410	3405.1							
	14	3342	3455	3393.8							
	15	3420	3340	3401.8							
	16	3370	3445	3394.3							
	17	3375	3425	3389.3							
	18	3435	3452	3387.6	1						
	21	3405	3432	3384.9	2						
	22	3377	3420	3380.6							
	23	3305	3387	3372.4							
	24	3215	3335	3360.4							
	25	3230	3360	3347.4							

Table 3. PORK BELLY METHOD TABULATION (Continued)

February Delivery − − 1968

Date 1967		Close	Deduct	10 Day Mov.Av.	Days Above/Below	100 Pts.	Price Bought	Con-tracts	Price Sold	Rule	Pts. Profit (Loss)
	28	3175	3342	3330.7							
	29	3082	3420	3296.9							
	30	3135	3370	3273.4							
	31	3200	3375	3255.9							
Sept.	1	3167	3435	3229.1							
	5	3177	3405	3206.3							
	6	3230	3377	3191.6	1						
	7	3195	3305	3180.6	2						
	8	3155	3215	3174.6							
	11	3160	3230	3167.6							
	12	3155	3175	3165.6							
	13	3210	3082	3178.4	1						
	14	3212	3135	3186.1	2						
	15	3195	3200	3185.6	3						
	18	3275	3167	3196.4	4						
	19	3257	3177	3204.4	5						
	20	3255	3230	3206.9							
	21	3310	3195	3218.4		x	3307	3		2	
	22	3342	3155	3237.1							
	25	3387	3160	3259.8				1	3407	4	100
	26	3382	3155	3282.5							
	27	3360	3210	3297.5							
	28	3375	3212	3313.8				2	3320	7	26
	29	3450	3195	3339.3							
Oct.	2	3477	3275	3359.5							
	3	3450	3257	3378.8							
	4	3520	3255	3405.3							
	5	3490	3310	3423.3							
	6	3485	3342	3437.6							
	9	3460	3387	3444.9							
	10	3350	3382	3441.7	1						
	11	3405	3360	3446.2	2						

Table 3. PORK BELLY METHOD TABULATION (Continued)

February Delivery — — 1968

Date 1967	Close	Deduct	10 Day Mov.Av.	Days Above/Below	100 Pts.	Price Bought	Con- tracts	Price Sold	Rule	Pts. Profit (Loss)
12	3450	3375	3453.7	3						
13	3442	3450	3452.9	4						
16	3375	3477	3442.7	5						———
								Profits to Date-------		1378

Table 3. PORK BELLY METHOD TABULATION (Continued)

February Delivery — — 1968

Date 1967	Close	Deduct	10 Day Mov.Av.	Days Above/Below	100 Pts.	Price Bought	Con- tracts	Price Sold	Rule	Pts. Profit (Loss)
Oct. 17	3417	3450	3439.4							
18	3367	3520	3424.1							
19	3345	3490	3409.6		x		3	3325	2	
20	3355	3485	3396.6							
23	3360	3460	3386.6							
24	3335	3350	3385.1							
25	3297	3405	3374.3							
26	3310	3450	3360.3							
27	3267	3442	3342.8							
30	3222	3375	3327.5			3225	1		4	100
31	3222	3417	3308.0							
Nov. 1	3242	3367	3295.5							
2	3225	3345	3283.5							
3	3195	3355	3267.5							
6	3242	3360	3255.7							
7	3265	3335	3248.7							
8	3232	3297	3242.2							
9	3197	3310	3230.9							
10	3200	3267	3224.2							
13	3265	3222	3228.5	1						

Table 3. PORK BELLY METHOD TABULATION (Continued)
February Delivery — — 1968

Date 1967		Close	Deduct	10 Day Mov.Av.	Days Above/Below	100 Pt.	Price Bought	Con-tracts	Price Sold	Rule	Pts. Profit (Loss)
	14	3235	3222	3229.8	2						
	15	3255	3242	3231.1	3						
	16	3340	3225	3242.6	4	x	3312	2		7	26
	17	3377	3195	3260.8	5		3377	3		2	
	20	3370	3242	3273.6							
	21	3355	3265	3282.6							
	22	3445	3232	3303.9							
	24	3452	3197	3329.4							
	27	3485	3200	3357.9				1	3477	4	100
	28	3420	3265	3373.4							
	29	3355	3235	3385.4				2	3390	7	26
	30	3360	3255	3395.9							
Dec.	1	3355	3340	3397.4							
	4	3380	3377	3397.7							
	5	3330	3370	3393.7							

Profits to Date------   1630

This completes all trades initiated in 1967

Profit Compilation

Gross profits 1630 points x $3 point = $4,890
Commissions on 13 completed trades =   1,404
Net Profits--------------------------------------- $3,486

None of this compilation is in any way guaranteed and no liability is assumed for its use.

21

HOW TO USE A COMPUTER
WITH MECHANICAL METHODS

Since the raw material for most mechanical methods is price and price alone, the natural assumption would be computers could do the job better than the statistician, if not better at least faster.

Years ago, when I was at a computer school, I talked one of my friends into just such an experiment. We decided to see if we could devise a mechanical system for soybean trading. It was a very interesting experience.

First, we had to pay a young lady to punch up about one thousand cards showing the high, low and close of a selected delivery of soybeans for the previous five years. Then we had to overlap these with a second delivery. In all, it took about two thousand cards.

Then, we had to program the computer, to instruct it what to do. It was a lot of work but interesting, nevertheless. After several false starts, we asked the computer these two basic questions:

1. Eliminating all moves of less than 10 cents from bottom to top or vice versa, how many moves of greater magnitude than 10 cents had taken place?

2. What were the various extent of such moves?

I think the answer to the first question was approximately an average of five a year and the extent of the moves varied from 10 1/8 cents to a high of 70 cents.

Well, now we knew a little something, so our next program was to get the 10-day moving average of that delivery of beans during the past five years. As I said earlier, we had to use two deliveries since one expired sometime during the year and had to be replaced by a second. The computer loved figuring that 10-day moving average. This was where it shone.

The next program was a little more complicated. We wanted to know the degree of truth shown by a penetration of the moving average: If the market sold 1 cent above the moving average, how far did the subsequent advance progress?

We received a lot of answers running all the way from 1/8 cent to 65 cents. Clearly, buying after a 1 cent penetration of the moving average was not the right move.

We increased the ante by 1/2 cent intervals all the way up to 10 cents and an analysis of our computer read-outs showed about 4 cents was the most satisfactory figure. This showed the smallest number of slight advances and the most satisfactory indications of a big move ahead. Therefore, we made our rule to read:

**Buy any time soybeans sell 4 cents above the previous day's
10 day moving average.**

An analysis of our read-out also dictated our profit-taking points at 10 cents and 15 cents. Stop loss points 4 cents below the moving average.

Take profits at 10 cents and 15 cents above cost.

But that took care of uptrends only. We had to ask the same questions in reverse for downward moves. Strangely, the computer came up with just about the same answers and stops. Sell 4 cents below the 10 day moving average, take profits at 10 cents and 15 cents. Stops 4 cents above the moving average.

Now, the method was ready for use. I opened a brokerage account with a local firm and began to use the method. It worked! I still have the first two confirmations showing profits of 10 cents and 15 cents.

Then, a strange thing happened. I lost interest in the method. I had proved it and that was that. I didn't need the money and my own business demanded 110 percent of my attention. I tried the method twice more and made a profit each time.

If you want to try it or research it, let me know how you come out. I will be interested.

Oh, one more thing. I don't know whether my friend ever used the method but he gave me a lasting respect for the IBM people. That man was easily one of the smartest young fellows I have met in a long time. That praise goes for almost everyone from IBM I've ever known. It's said IBM stands for It's Better Manually or I've Been Moved, but to me that B will always stand for Brains.

We know the computer can be very helpful in solving the niceties of mechanical trading.

For the last four years, our office has subscribed to a computer forecasting service. It is run by one of the largest commodity services in the country. We have had varying results with it but as a matter of interest for this book, I went back and collated the actual figures for the period of November 1967 to June 1970—about two and one-half years.

Here are a few of the approximate results using the computer service as an absolutely mechanical tool during that period (Illustration 21-1).

Commodity	Trades	Number of Profits	Losses	One Contract Profit
*Wheat	17	9	8	$ 1,019
Corn	13	7	6	862
*Oats	18	12	6	188
Soybeans	16	5	11	68

Commodity	Trades	Number of Profits	Losses	One Contract Profit
Pork Bellies	21	13	8	1,672
Cocoa	18	12	6	8,312
Cotton #2	12	7	5	5,050
*Copper	14	9	5	24,133

*See Tables 4, 5 and 6.

Illustration 21-1

While I do not guarantee any of these figures, they are reasonably accurate and have been figured after deducting approximate commission costs. Remember the copper totals cover the old 50,000 lb. contract. The new contract is for 25,000 lbs. and, thus, the results would have been about one-half the figure shown above if the new contract had been traded during that period.

The tabulation shows that the more volatile commodities seem to adapt better to computer speculation than do the more staid futures. However, as with all futures speculation, adequate money reserves *must* be kept against the inevitable large loss which will always occur at the worst possible time.

After much experience with this particular computer service, I believe it is programmed as if it were a great big chart. I have noticed the resistance points seem to be those shown on the bar chart. I believe they also use a moving average as a determinant of price direction. What other variables are programmed into their results are not known but there must be several others.

The poor results shown on several commodities are an indication of the trendless nature of their markets during the period under study. The computer, like any trend method, must not be caught too often in a trading range market. If it is, results like those shown for soybeans will occur. The last two great soybean markets were in 1966 and the late summer and fall of 1970—neither of which was covered by this study.

Before you throw all your hard-won knowledge of the commodity markets away and place all your faith in the computer, you should remember this method—like all others—has some built-in disadvantages. One of these is its losses tend to run in streaks. A tabulation will show you this tendency when using our same trading period (Illustration 21-2):

Commodity	Consecutive Losses Largest Number	Total $ Amount	Original Margin
Wheat	5	$ 781	$ 500
Corn	3	212	400
Oats	2	212	250
Soybeans	6	388	600

| | Consecutive Losses | | Original |
Commodity	Largest Number	Total $ Amount	Margin
Pork Bellies	3	2,481	1,000
Cocoa	3	1,125	900
Cotton #2	2	600	750
Copper	1	2,350	2,000

Illustration 21-2

You can see you are not going to have it all lavender and roses when using a computer method. I have not included commissions in this tabulation but they would add to the losses.

This also points up the absolute necessity of having backup money for your original margin. In every one of these cases, you would have been called upon to supply more money than your original stake. That is all well and good if you have already made a big profit but what if your first two or three trades are losses?

Do not, please, think I am overemphasizing the negative by my continual harping on money and losses. It is born of hard-won experience over many years. If you have money in reserve you have the power to last. If you do not, you are just another sucker waiting to be plucked by the market millionaires.

Table 4. COMPUTER RECORD ON WHEAT

| | Bought | | Sold | | Profit |
Delivery	Date	Price	Date	Price	(loss)
March	1-26-68	149 1/8	11-1-67	155 7/8	+ 6 3/4
May	3-13-68	153 5/8	3-20-68	148 1/2	− 5 1/8
July	5-23-68	139 1/2	4-2-68	147 5/8	+ 8 1/8
September	9-4-68	117	6-4-68	138 1/8	+21 1/8
March	10-14-68	132 3/4	11-20-68	134 1/2	+ 1 3/4
March	1-14-69	135 1/2	12-10-68	130 1/4	− 5 1/4
May	4-14-69	129 3/8	2-19-69	134 1/8	+ 4 3/4
July	4-25-69	131 3/8	5-26-69	128 1/2	− 2 7/8
September	8-7-69	123 7/8	6-13-69	130 1/4	+ 6 3/8
December	9-10-69	135	10-16-69	136 3/4	+ 1 3/4
March	11-11-69	139	12-15-69	142 5/8	+ 3 5/8
May	12-23-69	145 1/8	1-15-70	142	− 3 1/8
May	2-10-70	144 7/8	1-27-70	140 3/8	− 4 1/2
May	2-11-70	146 1/8	3-17-70	144 3/8	− 1 3/4
July	4-16-70	140 1/4	5-6-70	136 1/2	− 3 3/4

Table 4. COMPUTER RECORD ON WHEAT

| Delivery | Bought | | Sold | | Profit |
	Date	Price	Date	Price	(loss)
September	6-11-70	140 1/4	5-11-70	137 3/4	− 2 1/2
September	6-25-70	142 7/8	8-5-70	145 3/8	+ 2 1/2

Total----------------------------------	+27 7/8
27 7/8 x $50-----------------------	$1,393.75
Commissions (old rate)--------	374.00
Net Total----------------------------	$1,019.75

Table 5. COMPUTER RECORD ON OATS

| Delivery | Bought | | Sold | | Profit |
	Date	Price	Date	Price	Loss
May	12-8-67	71 1/2	3-15-69	72 3/8	+ 7/8
July	3-18-68	72 3/4	3-20-68	73 1/4	+ 1/2
July	3-28-68	74 1/2	4-15-68	70	− 4 1/2
July	5-23-68	71	4-22-68	71 1/2	+ 1/2
September	8-21-68	59 3/8	6-3-68	66 1/4	+ 6 7/8
December	9-16-68	63	10-24-68	66 1/8	+ 3 1/8
March	10-28-68	67 3/8	12-5-68	68 1/8	+ 3/8
May	1-3-69	70 3/4	2-10-69	72 1/8	+ 1 3/8
May	4-1-69	67 3/8	2-20-69	69 1/8	+ 1 3/4
July	4-15-69	67 3/4	5-14-69	64 3/8	− 3 3/8
September	7-7-69	62 3/4	5-28-69	64	+ 1 1/4
December	8-15-69	64 5/8	7-25-69	62 1/4	− 2 3/8
March	9-15-69	69 1/4	10-14-69	67 3/8	− 1 7/8
March	12-3-69	63	10-20-69	65 1/4	+ 2 1/4
March	1-6-70	64 3/8	12-4-69	62 1/2	− 1 7/8
May	3-2-70	61 7/8	1-20-70	65 3/8	+ 3 1/2
July	4-1-70	63 3/8	3-3-70	63 1/4	− 1/8
September	6-4-70	63 1/2	6-24-70	65 1/8	+ 1 5/8

Total---------------------------------	+10 1/4
10 1/8 x $50----------------------	$512.50
Commissions (old rate)--------	324.00
Net Total----------------------------	$188.50

Table 6. COMPUTER RECORD ON COPPER
(old contract)

Delivery	Bought Date	Bought Price	Sold Date	Sold Price	Profit Loss
March	12-12-67	57.85	1-23-68	60.50	+ 2.65
May	2-13-68	56.28	3-20-68	61.35	+ 5.07
July	5-24-68	46.00	3-26-68	52.40	+ 6.40
October	8-16-68	43.95	10-8-68	46.85	+ 2.90
January	11-8-68	46.85	1-7-69	51.65	+ 4.80
May	1-17-69	50.55	2-5-69	50.50	− 0.05
May	3-12-69	53.00	4-29-69	63.00	+10.00
September	5-27-69	56.90	6-26-69	56.90	--
September	7-16-69	60.95	9-2-69	71.65	+10.70
December	9-2-69	68.00	9-11-69	65.60	− 2.40
January	10-1-69	66.70	1-5-70	73.10	+ 6.40
March	2-6-70	72.00	1-15-70	67.30	− 4.70
May	2-11-70	69.95	4-25-70	74.05	+ 4.20
July	6-16-70	66.05	5-13-70	69.75	+ 3.70

Total--------------------------------   +49.67

4967 x $5-------------------------- $24,835

Commissions---------------------   702

Net Total-------------------------- $24,133

22

HOW TO USE OTHER MECHANICAL METHODS

I have often wondered at my interest in devising mechanical methods for trading in commodities. Why don't I try to use the fundamentals which made so much money for my father and grandfather?

Well, in the first place, I don't have their basic knowledge of one certain commodity. They specialized in lard when lard was a big market on the Chicago Board of Trade. They knew everything—or hoped they did—about the lard market. In addition, they were brokers for one of the big packing houses so they had much information regarding the physical commodity and internal trade conditions as well as the futures. You might say they ate, drank and slept with the lard market—and with very favorable results. Their old firm is still functioning as a subsidiary of the packing house for whom they were brokers so long ago.

But the average commodity trader is not a member of the Chicago Board of Trade and he does not have access to any specialized information. He has only himself and the advice of his broker. After a few experiences with this type of well-meant advice, he knows enough to realize he must have a more solid base for his trading or give it up entirely. That is the reason I first went into mechanical methods and that is the reason I still use them for a great deal of my customers' trading.

In previous chapters, I have outlined my use of mechanical methods for trading in pork bellies and soybeans. These are both based on moving averages to determine the trend.

There are other ways of using moving averages for this purpose. Some methods are combinations of two or more averages, others are based on them occurring in a certain progression, some use the total of all the averages. Let us examine a few of these ideas.

The first and most used method of manipulating these averages is to take two of them, one a 10 day average and the other a 20 day. Plotting these, the trader would buy when the 10 day exceeded the 20 day and sell if the reverse took place (Illustration 22-1):

Day	10 day average	20 day average
Monday	54.6	55.9
Tuesday	54.7	56.0

125

Day	10 day average	20 day average
Wednesday	54.8	56.1
Thursday	57.0	56.3

Illustration 22-1

Thus, you would get a signal to buy Thursday at the close or on the opening Friday. You would use exactly the same technique to sell short when the 10 day average dipped below the 20 day.

This method, or its modifications, has a number of adherents. My main objection to it is the likelihood of whipsaws—say that Friday's 10 day total was 56.2 and the 20 day was 56.3 indicating a sell signal right after you had bought the previous day.

Another way of using the averages is to take the average for the last ten days, the previous ten days and the ten days previous to that and to buy or sell when these figures arranged themselves in a declining or increasing trend, thus (Illustration 22-2):

Day	Last 10 day average	1st previous 10 day average	2nd previous 10 day average
Monday	354	346	352
Tuesday	355	347	351
Wednesday	355	347	350
Thursday	356	348	349
Friday	357	349	348

Illustration 22-2

Using this method, you would conclude that this arrangement of the averages forecasts a rising market. The nearest average is above the next nearest and that, in turn, is above the oldest. All the ducks are in a row, ready for shooting.

This idea has the merit of being very simple but it will probably work only on very trendful commodities since by the time all the averages have fallen into their appointed places, the move may be over. Just as an example, you can check it against the sugar tables (Table 8), even though we are using them to show another method.

The first sale using the above idea would be on January 23 followed by a purchase on May 6 and a subsequent sale on May 31.

A variation of this plan and the one we are illustrating by using the sugar tables is as follows:

You take a position when the *sum* of the three averages reverses itself, as on January 11 and January 23.

A three contract position is taken at the close of that day.

Once a position is taken, it is held for at least four following days. If, at that time, the trend of the averages has reversed, the position is closed out and a new position taken according to the new trend. This, too, must meet the four day test.

Profit taking orders for one contract each are placed 20, 30 and 40 points from the trade price.

Stop loss orders on all three contracts are placed 20 points against the trade price. When the first 20 point profit has been taken, the stop orders on the remaining contracts are adjusted to the trade price plus commission (about 4 points).

Please examine the tables. The first trade was on January 11, when three contracts were bought. These were closed out on January 25 at a small profit and, in addition, three contracts were sold short. Our new position had profit taking orders at 260, 250 and 240 for one contract each and a stop loss order for three contracts at 300.

The first profit was taken on February 3. The stop loss orders at 300 were immediately cancelled and we placed a two contract stop order at 276 (280 −4 points commission).

The next profit was achieved on February 20. The stop order was accordingly changed to only one contract at 276. The last profit was taken at 240 on February 23. The remaining stop was cancelled as all three contracts had been completed.

On May 8, we go long three contracts at 216. Profit taking orders are placed at 236, 246 and 256. Stop loss orders on all three contracts at 196 (216 −20).

The first profit is taken on May 20 and the stops on the remaining two contracts changed from 196 to 220 (216 + 4 points). This stop is hit on May 24 and the last two contracts closed out to complete the transaction with a gross profit of 28 points less commission.

This method showed good gains in 1967 and 1968, a small gain in 1969 and a loss in 1970. Overall, the four year results were quite satisfactory.

As I pointed out in my chapter on the pork belly method, you should *always* back-check any mechanical method for at least four years. I like my profit years to have averaged 100 percent of margin or better so that the sum of the net total for the four years averages at least 200 percent on original margin or about 50 percent per year overall. You will usually find that a good mechanical method has two profitable years out of four, one barely profitable year and one loss year. If, say, the profit years show about 180 percent, 20 percent and 140 percent on original margin and your loss year a minus 100 percent, you will have an overall profit of 240 percent or about 60 percent year for the four years. Of course, all commissions should be deducted before you figure profits and—additionally—you should always have extra margin money.

As for back-checking, your public library usually has the daily paper on microfilm or in a letter press. *The Wall Street Journal* is also usually available on microfilm in the big city library. The best source, of course, is to keep a daily file of the commodity page of *The Wall Street Journal.* Start one today.

Table 7. TRIPLE AVERAGE SUGAR METHOD TABULATION
SUGAR #8
September 1968 Delivery

1968 Date	Low of Close	Deduct	Last 10 Day Total	1st 10 Prev. Days	2nd 10 Prev. Days	30 Day Total	No. of Contracts	Buy Price	Sell Price	Profit (Loss)
1-3	274	285	2852	2709	2652	8213				
1-4	269	278	2843	2737	2623	8203				
1-5	269	285	2827	2770	2595	8192				
1-8	266	290	2803	2798	2585	8186				
1-9	264	289	2778	2814	2593	8185				
1-10	267	285	2760	2831	2587	8178				
1-11	274	288	2746	2838	2600	8184	3	274		
1-12	270	295	2721	2853	2616	8190				
1-15	263	386	2698	2855	2650	8203				
1-16	264	282	2680	2863	2678	8211				
1-17	273	274	2679	2852	2709	8240				
1-18	277	269	2687	2843	2737	8267				
1-19	277	269	2695	2827	2770	8292				
1-22	274	266	2703	2803	2798	8304				
1-23	276	264	2715	2778	2814	8307				
1-24	277	267	2725	2760	2831	8316				
1-25	280	274	2731	2746	2838	8315	6		280	+ 18
1-26	276	270	2737	2721	2853	8311				
1-29	266	263	2740	2698	2855	8293				
1-30	268	264	2744	2680	2863	8287				
1-31	269	273	2740	2679	2852	8271				
2-1	271	277	2734	2687	2843	8264				
2-2	267	277	2724	2695	2827	8246				
2-3	260	274	2710	2703	2803	8216	1	260		+ 20
2-6	259	276	2693	2715	2778	8186				
2-7	261	277	2677	2725	2760	8162				
2-8	266	280	2663	2731	2746	8140				
2-9	262	276	2649	2737	2721	8107				
2-13	251	266	2634	2740	2698	8072				
2-14	254	268	2620	2744	2680	8044				
2-15	256	269	2607	2740	2679	8026				

Table 7. TRIPLE AVERAGE SUGAR METHOD TABULATION (Continued)

SUGAR #8
September 1968 Delivery

1968 Date	Low of Close	Deduct	Last 10 Day Total	1st 10 Prev. Days	2nd 10 Prev. Days	30 Day Total	No. of Contracts	Buy Price	Sell Price	Profit (Loss)
2-16	258	271	2594	2734	2687	8015				
2-19	254	267	2581	2724	2695	8000				
2-20	246	260	2567	2710	2703	7980	1	250		+ 30
2-21	245	259	2553	2693	2715	7961				
2-23	238	261	2530	2677	2725	7932	1	240		+ 40
2-26	240	266	2504	2663	2731	7898				
2-27	237	262	2479	2649	2737	7865				
2-28	243	251	2471	2634	2740	7845				
2-29	242	254	2459	2620	2744	7823				
3-1	239	256	2442	2607	2740	7789				
3-4	230	258	2414	2594	2734	7742				
3-5	228	254	2388	2581	2724	7693				
3-6	224	246	2366	2567	2710	7643				
3-7	231	245	2352	2553	2693	7598				
3-8	231	238	2345	2530	2677	7552				
3-11	233	240	2338	2504	2663	7505				
3-12	230	237	2331	2479	2649	7459				
3-13	235	243	2323	2471	2634	7428				
3-14	241	242	2322	2459	2620	7401				
3-15	240	239	2323	2442	2607	7372				
3-18	231	230	2324	2414	2594	7332				
3-19	229	228	2325	2388	2581	7294				
3-20	233	224	2334	2366	2567	7267				
3-21	226	231	2329	2352	2553	7234				
3-22	222	231	2320	2345	2530	7195				
3-25	212	233	2299	2338	2504	7141				
3-26	217	230	2286	2331	2479	7096				
3-27	212	235	2263	2323	2471	7057				
3-28	212	241	2234	2322	2459	7015				
3-29	219	240	2213	2323	2442	6978				
4-1	216	231	2198	2324	2414	6936				

Table 7. TRIPLE AVERAGE SUGAR METHOD TABULATION (Continued)
SUGAR #8
September 1968 Delivery

1968 Date	Low of Close	Deduct	Last 10 Day Total	1st 10 Prev. Days	2nd 10 Prev. Days	30 Day Total	No. of Contracts	Buy Price	Sell Price	Profit (Loss)
4-2	214	229	2183	2325	2308	6896				
4-3	207	233	2157	2334	2366	6857				
4-4	204	226	2135	2329	2352	6816				
4-5	205	222	2118	2320	2345	6783				
4-8	204	212	2110	2299	2338	6747				
4-10	211	217	2104	2286	2331	6721				
4-11	215	212	2107	2263	2323	6693				
4-15	217	212	2112	2234	2322	6668				
4-16	213	219	2106	2213	2323	6642				
4-17	227	216	2117	2198	2324	6639				
4-18	228	214	2131	2183	2325	6639				
4-19	222	207	2146	2157	2334	6637				
4-22	226	204	2168	2135	2329	6632				
4-23	229	205	2192	2118	2320	6630				
4-24	229	204	2217	2110	2299	6626				
4-25	227	211	2233	2104	2286	6623				
4-26	230	215	2248	2107	2263	6618				
4-29	224	217	2255	2112	2234	6601				
4-30	218	213	2260	2106	2213	6579				
5-1	214	227	2247	2117	2198	6562				
5-2	219	228	2238	2131	2183	6552				
5-3	222	222	2238	2146	2157	6541				
5-6	220	226	2232	2168	2135	6535				
5-7	219	229	2222	2192	2118	6532				
5-8	216	229	2209	2217	2110	6536	3	216		
5-9	223	227	2205	2233	2104	6542				
5-10	220	230	2195	2248	2107	6550				
5-13	222	224	2193	2255	2112	6560				
5-14	227	218	2202	2260	2106	6568				

Table 7. TRIPLE AVERAGE SUGAR METHOD TABULATION (Continued)
SUGAR #8
September 1968 Delivery

1968 Date	Low of Close	Deduct	Last 10 Day Total	1st 10 Prev. Days	2nd 10 Prev. Days	30 Day Total	No. of Contracts	Buy Price	Sell Price	Profit (Loss)
5-15	233	214	2221	2247	2117	6585				
5-16	229	219	2231	2238	2131	6595				
5-17	229	222	2238	2238	2146	6622				
5-20	236	220	2254	2232	2168	6654	1		236	+ 20
5-21	232	219	2267	2222	2192	6681				
5-22	225	216	2276	2209	2217	6702				
5-23	225	223	2278	2205	2233	6716				
5-24	223	220	2281	2195	2248	6724	2		220	+ 8
5-27	222	222	2281	2193	2255	6729				
5-28	216	227	2270	2202	2260	6732				
5-29	213	233	2250	2221	2247	6718	3		213	
5-31	204	229	2225	2231	2238	6694				
6-3	194	229	2190	2238	2238	6666	1	193		+ 20
6-4	196	236	2150	2254	2232	6636				
6-5	207	232	2125	2267	2222	6614				
6-6	209	225	2109	2276	2209	6594				
6-7	204	225	2088	2278	2205	6571				
6-10	196	223	2061	2281	2195	6537				
6-11	196	222	2035	2281	2193	6509				
6-12	197	216	2016	2270	2202	6488				
6-13	196	213	1999	2250	2221	6470				
6-14	201	204	1996	2225	2231	6452				
6-17	192	194	1994	2190	2238	6422				
6-18	195	196	1993	2150	2254	6397				
6-19	196	207	1984	2125	2267	6376				
6-20	204	209	1979	2109	2276	6364				
6-21	201	204	1976	2088	2278	6342				
6-24	204	196	1984	2061	2281	6326				
6-25	198	196	1986	2035	2281	6302				
6-26	192	197	1981	2016	2270	6267				

Table 7. TRIPLE AVERAGE SUGAR METHOD TABULATION (Continued)

SUGAR #8

September 1968 Delivery

1968 Date	Low of Close	Deduct	Last 10 Day Total	1st 10 Prev. Days	2nd 10 Prev. Days	30 Day Total	No. of Contracts	Buy Price	Sell Price	Profit (Loss)
6-27	185	196	1970	1999	2250	6219				
6-28	189	201	1958	1996	2225	6179	1	183		+ 30
7-1	186	192	1952	1994	2190	6136				
7-2	193	195	1950	1993	2150	6093				
7-3	194	196	1948	1984	2125	6057				
7-8	190	204	1934	1979	2109	6022				
7-9	183	201	1916	1976	2088	5980				
7-10	180	204	1892	1984	2061	5937				
7-11	178	198	1872	1986	2035	5893				
Contract expired 8-13			Price at expiration				1		173	+ 40

SUGAR #8

March 1969 Delivery

1968 Date	Low of Close	Deduct	Last 10 Day Total	1st 10 Prev. Days	2nd 10 Prev. Days	30 Day Total	No. of Contracts	Buy Price	Sell Price	Profit (Loss)
7-12	232	240	2354	2442	2406	7202				
7-15	233	235	2353	2436	2395	7184				
7-16	239	238	2354	2428	2401	7183				
7-17	233	235	2352	2423	2407	7182				
7-18	234	243	2343	2423	2416	7182				
7-19	233	240	2336	2419	2414	7169				
7-22	240	238	2338	2407	2419	7164				
7-23	235	233	2340	2394	2422	7156				
7-24	235	232	2343	2378	2434	7155				
7-25	237	229	2351	2362	2441	7154				
7-26	238	232	2357	2354	2442	7153				
7-29	229	233	2353	2353	2436	7142				

Table 7. TRIPLE AVERAGE SUGAR METHOD TABULATION (Continued)

SUGAR #8

March 1969 Delivery

1968 Date	Low of Close	Deduct	Last 10 Day Total	1st 10 Prev. Days	2nd 10 Prev. Days	30 Day Total	No. of Contracts	Buy Price	Sell Price	Profit (Loss)
7-30	232	239	2346	2354	2428	7128				
7-31	230	233	2343	2352	2423	7118				
8-1	233	234	2342	2343	2423	7108				
8-2	236	233	2345	2336	2419	7100				
8-5	235	240	2340	2338	2407	7085				
8-6	237	235	2342	2340	2394	7076				
8-7	232	235	2339	2343	2378	7060				
8-8	229	237	2331	2351	2362	7044				
8-9	225	238	2328	2357	2354	7039				
8-12	227	229	2326	2353	2353	7032				
8-13	222	232	2316	2346	2354	7016				
8-14	221	230	2307	2343	2352	7002				
8-15	223	233	2297	2342	2343	6982				
8-16	223	236	2284	2345	2336	6965				
8-19	224	235	2273	2340	2338	6951				
8-20	224	237	2260	2342	2340	6942				
8-21	222	232	2250	2339	2343	6932				
8-22	219	229	2240	2331	2351	6922				
8-23	212	225	2227	2328	2357	6912				
8-24	204	227	2204	2326	2353	6883				
8-27	201	222	2183	2316	2346	6845				
8-28	203	221	2165	2307	2343	6815				
8-29	207	223	2149	2297	2342	6788				
8-30	205	223	2131	2284	2345	6760				
9-3	189	224	2096	2273	2340	6709				
9-4	189	224	2061	2260	2342	6663				
9-5	195	222	2034	2250	2339	6623				
9-6	192	219	2007	2240	2331	6518				
9-9	186	212	1981	2227	2328	6536				
9-10	181	204	1948	2204	2326	6478				
9-11	187	201	1934	2183	2316	6433				

Table 7. TRIPLE AVERAGE SUGAR METHOD TABULATION (Continued)

SUGAR #8

March 1969 Delivery

1968 Date	Low of Close	Deduct	Last 10 Day Total	1st 10 Prev. Days	2nd 10 Prev. Days	30 Day Total	No. of Contracts	Buy Price	Sell Price	Profit (Loss)
9-12	187	203	1918	2165	2307	6390				
9-13	181	207	1892	2149	2297	6338				
9-16	188	205	1875	2131	2284	6290				
9-17	189	189	1875	2096	2273	6244				
9-18	190	189	1876	2061	2260	6207				
9-19	199	195	1880	2034	2250	6164				
9-20	198	192	1886	2007	2240	6133				
9-23	194	186	1894	1981	2227	6102				
9-24	204	181	1917	1948	2204	6069				
9-25	208	187	1938	1934	2183	6055				
9-26	199	187	1950	1918	2165	6033				
9-27	207	181	1976	1892	2149	6017				
9-30	202	188	1990	1875	2131	5996				
10-1	197	189	1996	1875	2096	5969				
10-2	199	190	2007	1876	2061	5944				
10-3	200	199	2008	1880	2034	5922				
10-4	195	198	2005	1886	2007	5898				
10-7	197	194	2008	1894	1981	5883				
10-8	194	204	1998	1917	1948	5863				
10-9	198	208	1988	1938	1934	5860				
10-10	206	199	1995	1950	1918	5863	3	206		
10-11	218	207	2006	1976	1892	5874				
10-14	212	202	2016	1990	1875	5881				
10-15	219	197	2038	1998	1875	5911				
10-16	226	199	2065	2007	1876	5948	1		226	+ 20
10-17	225	200	2090	2008	1880	5978				
10-18	233	195	2128	2005	1886	6019	1		236	+ 30
10-21	236	197	2167	2008	1894	6069				
10-22	252	194	2225	1998	1917	6140	1		246	+ 40
10-23	263	198	2290	1988	1938	6216				
10-24	255	206	2339	1995	1950	6284				

Table 7. TRIPLE AVERAGE SUGAR METHOD TABULATION (Continued)

SUGAR #8

March 1969 Delivery

1968 Date	Low of Close	Deduct	Last 10 Day Total	1st 10 Prev. Days	2nd 10 Prev. Days	30 Day Total	No. of Contracts	Buy Price	Sell Price	Profit (Loss)
10-25	255	218	2376	2006	1976	6358				
10-28	255	212	2419	2016	1990	6425				
10-29	266	219	2466	2038	1998	6502				
10-30	277	226	2515	2065	2007	6587				
10-31	276	225	2566	2090	2008	6664				
11-1	269	233	2602	2128	2005	6735				
11-4	277	236	2643	2167	2008	6818				
11-6	276	252	2667	2225	1998	6890				
11-7	277	263	2681	2290	1988	6959				
11-8	279	255	2705	2339	1995	7039				
11-12	270	255	2720	2376	2006	7102				
11-13	265	255	2730	2419	2016	7165				
11-14	287	266	2751	2466	2038	7255				
11-15	295	277	2769	2515	2065	7349				
11-18	305	276	2798	2566	2090	7454				
11-19	300	269	2829	2602	2128	7559				
11-20	302	277	2854	2643	2167	7664				
11-21	297	276	2875	2667	2225	7767				
11-22	297	277	2895	2681	2290	7866				
11-25	296	279	2912	2705	2339	7956				
11-26	297	270	2939	2720	2376	8035				
11-27	310	265	2984	2730	2419	8133				
11-29	313	287	3010	2751	2466	8227				
12-2	310	295	3025	2769	2515	8309				
12-3	309	305	3029	2798	2566	8393				
12-4	309	300	3038	2829	2602	8469				
12-5	315	302	3051	2854	2643	8548				
12-6	311	297	3065	2875	2667	8607				
12-9	308	297	3076	2895	2681	8652				
12-10	296	296	3076	2912	2705	8693				
12-11	303	297	3082	2939	2720	8741				

Table 7. TRIPLE AVERAGE SUGAR METHOD TABULATION (Continued)

SUGAR #8

March 1969 Delivery

1968 Date	Low of Close	Deduct	Last 10 Day Total	1st 10 Prev. Days	2nd 10 Prev. Days	30 Day Total	No. of Contracts	Buy Price	Sell Price	Profit (Loss)
12-12	308	310	3080	2984	2730	8794				
12-13	303	313	3070	3010	2751	8831				
12-16	297	310	3057	3025	2769	8851				
12-17	297	309	3045	3029	2798	8872				
12-18	297	309	3033	3038	2829	8900				
12-19	299	315	3017	3051	2854	8922				
12-20	301	311	3007	3065	2875	8947				
12-23	314	308	3013	3076	2895	8984				
12-24	313	296	3030	3082	2912	9024				
12-26	309	303	3036	3080	2939	9055				
12-27	312	308	3040	3070	2984	9094				
12-28	308	303	3045	3057	3010	9112				
12-31	308	297	3056	3045	3025	9126				

Gross Statistical Profit---------------------------------- + 316

Less Commissions (Approx.)------------------------ − 48

Net Statistical Profit (Approx.)-------------------- + 268

N.B. This tabulation is in no way guaranteed and no liability is assumed for its use. This is a statistical summary only compiled from past records.

23

HOW TO USE TRADING VOLUME

Thus far we have looked at the market through the eyes of price and, for the most part, price alone.

One of the most famous and successful stock market indicators combines price change times volume. What if we were to do the same thing on commodity futures? Would we have a good method of price forecasting?

To get the idea of what would happen, I compiled yearly tables in which I multiplied the daily price change of a delivery of pork bellies times the total volume for that day (brought to its nearest thousand). I then compiled a running total of these results and formed that total into a 10 day moving average.

When that average changed direction, I bought or sold on paper in the direction of the change. I would take a three contract position and liquidate it at profits of 100, 200 and 300 points or at the price where the trend changed if this occurred before the final profit point.

My results were good—impressive in 1967 and 1969 but only about even in 1968.

Let's look at Table 8 and I will go over it with you.

Table 8.   PORK BELLY FUTURES TABLE

May 1969 Delivery

Date	Price Change	Volume	+ Balance	− Forward	Change Total	11th Day Deduct	10 Day Average
1-1-69					− 0.22		
1-2	− 0.10	3		0.30	− 0.52		
1-3	− 0.38	4		1.52	− 2.04		
1-6	+ 0.32	3	0.96		− 1.08		
1-7	− 0.20	3		0.60	− 1.68		
1-8	+ 0.45	4	1.80		+ 0.12		
1-9	− 0.15	4		0.60	− 0.48		
1-10	0.00	2	0	0	− 0.48		

Table 8.   PORK BELLY FUTURES TABLE (Continued)
May 1969 Delivery

Date	Price Change	Volume	+ Balance	– Forward	Change Total	11th Day Deduct	10 Day Average
1-13	+ 0.58	4	2.32		+ 1.84		
1-14	+ 0.10	5	0.50		+ 2.34		– 1.90
1-15	+ 0.82	9	7.38		+ 9.72	– 0.22	+ 8.04
1-16	– 0.15	6		0.90	+ 8.82	– 0.52	+17.38
1-17	– 0.47	7		3.29	+ 5.53	– 2.04	+24.95
1-20	0.00	3	0	0	+ 5.53	– 1.08	+31.56
1-21	+ 0.45	5	2.25		+ 7.78	– 1.68	+41.02
1-22	– 0.40	5		2.00	+ 5.78	+ 0.12	+46.68
1-23	+ 0.50	8	4.00		+ 9.78	– 0.48	+56.94
1-24	– 0.18	5		0.90	+ 8.88	– 0.48	+66.30
1-27	+ 0.10	5	0.50		+ 9.38	+ 1.84	+73.84
1-28	– 0.10	5		0.50	+ 8.88	+ 2.34	+80.38
1-29	– 0.07	5		0.35	+ 8.53	+ 9.72	+79.19
1-30	– 0.40	7		2.80	+ 5.73	+ 8.82	+76.10
1-31	– 0.10	6		0.60	+ 5.13	+ 5.53	+75.70
2-3	+ 0.05	5	0.25		+ 5.38	+ 5.53	+75.55
2-4	+ 0.15	4	0.60		+ 5.88	+ 7.78	+73.65
2-5	– 0.03	4		0.12	+ 5.76	+ 5.78	+73.63
2-6	+ 0.07	4	0.28		+ 6.04	+ 9.78	+69.89
2-7	+ 0.63	8	5.04		+11.08	+ 8.88	+72.09
2-10	– 0.08	6		0.48	+10.60	+ 9.38	+73.31
2-11	– 0.02	6		0.12	+10.48	+ 8.88	+74.91
2-12	+ 0.22	6	1.32		+11.80	+ 8.53	+78.18
2-13	– 0.20	4		0.80	+11.00	+ 5.73	+83.45
2-14	+ 0.53	4	2.12		+13.12	+ 5.13	+91.04
2-17	+ 0.60	10	6.00		+19.12	+ 5.38	+104.78
2-18	+ 1.40	11	15.40		+34.52	+ 5.88	+133.42
2.19	– 0.40	7		2.80	+31.72	+ 5.76	+159.38
2.20	+ 0.62	9	5.58		+37.30	+ 6.04	+190.64
2.24	+ 0.55	9	4.95		+42.25	+11.08	+221.81

Price change: I usually take the lowest amount of change. If the price shows a range of, say, "–.05 to unchanged," I invariably take the unchanged and note it as "0" change, as shown on January 20.

Volume is total volume to nearest thousand, up or down. 2,300 would be shown as 2, while 4565 would be shown as 5.

+ or − is total of price change times volume.

Change total is the running total of price changes. You can start this with 0 if you wish; it is the daily changes that dictate the trend.

11th day deduct is used to keep the 10 day average intact. You always deduct the 11th preceding day when compiling a 10 day average.

10 day average is the sum of the change totals for the last ten days. Note, if your average is a plus, your change total is a plus but your 11th day deduct is a minus, then this minus is added to the total, not subtracted from it, as shown on January 16.

I have used the table to illustrate the changes in trends. Closing prices are used for our paper results.

On January 15, we are still in an upward trend, the 10 day average is improving. This continues until January 29, when the 10 day trend starts to slip.

On February 5, the trend is nearly reversed but we have to wait until February 7 for the real reversal to show up and the start of a real rise begins.

If you had been trading on this method, you would have bought on January 10 at 32.40, taken a 100 point profit at 33.40 on January 15 and sold the others out and gone short at about 33.50 on January 29.

On February 7, you would buy in your shorts at a 150 point loss on three contracts and go long at about 34.00, taking a 100 point profit on February 17, 200 points on February 18 and 300 points on February 24.

Thus, on your three trades you would have shown a paper profit of about 770 points ($2,320 at the old rates) before commissions of $324 (all figured at the old rates). The rate per point on pork bellies now is $3.60 per contract and the commissions are $45 round turn per contract.

Yet, this method is not all beer and skittles. Daily reversals are encountered which eat up commission money and also may show losses. Look at the tabulation for February 5. If the change had been 5.80 instead of 5.76, the market would have signaled an uptrend, only to be reversed the next day and *that* figure to be finally reversed the next day for a total of three trades in three days.

The trader might eliminate this annoyance by saying he would not change his position unless his match against the nearest three deduct days was correct.

Thus, on January 29, he would not have changed positions since he had this situation:

$$+ 2.34$$
$$+ 8.53 \quad + 9.72$$
$$+ 8.82$$

+ 8.53 below both + 9.72 and + 8.82 but was not below + 2.34 so the cautious trader would have waited until February 3 to go short since at that time—

$$+ 5.53$$
$$+ 5.38 \quad + 5.53$$
$$+ 7.78$$

clearly showed a downtrend as all the 11 day deducts were greater than the daily change for February 3.

This delay would have cost him about 45 points per contract but would have prevented most whipsaws due to the daily change.

Again, when the trend finally changed on February 7, we had this compilation:

$$+ 9.78$$
$$+ 11.08 + 8.88$$
$$+ 9.38$$

showing a clear reversal in the direction of the trend.

The reader should, however, be cautioned about making such changes in a method. They rarely give better results. It is possible to so refine a method no trades will be made or perhaps one trade a year. The overall profit picture usually goes down whenever you try to make a method too safe.

All methods have their good and bad years. You may get a good trend method and run into a trading range market which will get you long at the top and short on the bottom. There is nothing you can do except follow through faithfully according to your method, take your losses and hope the trend will be resumed before you run out of money!

24

HOW TO TRADE ON THE FUTURES INDEX

As every reader knows, the Dow Jones stock averages are quoted daily and show the general direction in which the market is headed. It should be stressed these are averages. In even the worst days of decline, certain stocks advance against the trend and on the days when everything is going sky-high, there are always laggards which go down instead of up. Yet the averages give the public an idea of the market's general direction and as such are quite valuable indicators.

The Dow Jones Commodity Futures Index* serves the same function in the commodity markets. It is an average of the futures prices of about eight to twelve commodities and, thus, is an index of the general trend of those markets as a whole.

I did not pay too much attention to this average during my first years in the commodity markets. It did not seem to adapt itself to my purpose which was, always, *to find and follow a trend* in an individual commodity. Yet, subsequent research has given me several ways in which this average may be used.

Referring to Tables 9 through 11, you will see a weekly compilation of the Index for the years 1968, 1969 and 1970, together with a 10 week moving average of those figures.

Table 9. DOW JONES COMMODITY FUTURES INDEX

(10 week moving average)

1968

Date	Index	Deduct	M. A.	Date	Index	Deduct	M. A.
1-2	141.79	135.52	141.93	2-4	142.03	144.20	142.62
1-9	142.30	136.81	142.48	2-13	138.34	145.46	141.91
1-15	141.59	138.03	142.83	2-19	139.10	144.25	141.39
1-22	140.94	140.22	142.90	2-26	139.53	143.63	140.98
1-29	142.06	142.73	142.84	3-4	140.35	142.19	140.80

Table 9. DOW JONES COMMODITY FUTURES INDEX   (Continued)
(10 week moving average)

1968 Date	Index	Deduct	M.A.	Date	Index	Deduct	M.A.
3-19	140.54	141.79	140.67	8-12	134.09	136.84	135.29
3-25	138.56	142.30	140.30	8-19	133.96	135.57	135.12
4-1	138.14	141.59	139.95	8-26	133.86	135.54	134.95
4-8	137.13	140.94	139.57	8-30	134.27	135.59	134.82
4-15	135.46	142.06	138.91	9-9	135.54	135.17	134.85
4-22	136.16	142.03	138.33	9-16	134.82	134.91	134.84
4-29	136.06	138.34	138.10	9-23	135.73	136.82	134.74
5-6	135.67	139.10	137.76	9-30	134.87	137.00	134.52
5-13	135.81	139.53	137.38	10-7	136.67	134.52	134.74
5-20	136.39	140.35	136.99	10-14	138.03	133.51	135.19
5-27	136.94	140.54	136.63	10-21	137.99	134.09	135.58
6-3	136.84	138.56	136.46	10-28	138.81	133.96	136.06
6-10	135.67	138.14	136.21	11-4	140.96	133.86	136.77
6-17	135.54	137.13	136.05	11-11	142.29	134.27	137.58
6-24	135.59	135.46	136.06	11-18	144.17	135.54	138.44
7-1	135.17	136.16	135.96	11-25	142.27	134.82	139.18
7-8	134.91	136.06	135.85	12-2	142.75	135.73	139.89
7-15	136.82	135.67	135.96	12-9	143.60	134.87	140.76
7-22	137.00	135.81	136.09	12-16	144.54	136.67	141.55
7-29	134.52	136.39	135.91	12-23	143.20	138.03	142.06
8-5	133.51	136.94	135.56	12-30	142.82	137.99	142.54

Table 10. DOW JONES COMMODITY FUTURES INDEX
(10 week moving average)

1969 Date	Index	Deduct	M. A.	Date	Index	Deduct	M. A.
1-6	144.42	138.81	143.10	2-3	140.80	142.27	142.62
1-13	142.38	140.96	143.24	2-10	138.01	142.75	142.14
1-20	140.15	142.29	143.03	2-17	138.57	143.60	141.64
1-27	141.56	144.17	142.76	2-24	139.99	144.54	141.19

Table 10. DOW JONES COMMODITY FUTURES INDEX (Continued)

(10 week moving average)

1969 Date	Index	Deduct	M.A.	Date	Index	Deduct	M.A.
3-3	139.08	143.20	140.77	8-4	138.88	138.51	139.30
3-10	139.18	142.82	140.41	8-11	139.48	138.89	139.36
3-17	137.85	144.42	139.76	8-18	139.74	138.82	139.45
3-24	137.37	142.38	139.26	8-25	140.49	138.27	139.67
4-1	138.31	140.15	139.08	9-2	139.50	139.22	139.70
4-7	138.58	141.56	138.78	9-8	139.69	138.17	139.85
4-14	139.63	140.80	138.66	9-15	141.35	140.71	139.92
4-22	139.02	138.01	138.76	9-22	141.18	140.84	139.95
4-29	139.53	138.57	138.86	9-29	141.19	140.92	139.98
5-5	139.94	139.99	138.85	10-6	141.60	138.20	140.32
5-12	140.20	139.08	138.97	10-13	141.97	138.88	140.63
5-19	139.88	139.18	139.04	10-20	142.40	139.48	140.92
5-26	138.51	137.85	139.10	10-27	142.51	139.74	141.20
6-2	138.89	136.37	139.26	11-3	143.38	140.49	141.48
6-9	138.82	138.31	139.31	11-10	144.05	139.50	141.94
6-16	138.27	138.58	139.28	11-17	141.72	139.69	142.14
6-23	139.22	139.63	139.23	11-24	141.67	141.35	142.17
6-30	138.17	139.02	139.15	12-1	141.63	141.18	142.22
7-7	140.71	139.53	139.27	12-8	141.92	141.19	142.29
7-14	140.84	139.94	139.36	12-15	141.31	141.60	142.26
7-21	140.92	140.20	139.43	12-22	140.25	141.97	142.09
7-28	138.20	139.88	139.26	12-30	139.12	142.40	141.76

Table 11. DOW JONES COMMODITY FUTURES INDEX

(10 week moving average)

1970 Date	Index	Deduct	M. A.	1970 Date	Index	Deduct	M. A.
1-5	138.56	142.51	141.36	2-9	135.25	141.63	138.48
1-12	137.47	143.38	140.77	2-16	135.86	141.92	137.87
1-19	137.46	144.05	140.11	2-23	135.92	141.31	137.33
1-26	136.79	141.72	139.61	3-2	134.07	140.25	136.72
2-2	136.71	141.67	139.12	3-9	134.01	139.12	136.21

Table 11. DOW JONES COMMODITY FUTURES INDEX (Continued)

(10 week moving average)

1970 Date	Index	Deduct	M.A.	1970 Date	Index	Deduct	M.A.
3-16	134.01	138.56	135.76	8-10	140.29	134.87	136.63
3-23	134.42	137.47	135.45	8-17	145.27	133.94	137.77
3-30	133.91	137.46	135.10	8-25	143.83	135.91	138.56
4-6	134.54	136.79	134.87	8-31	146.38	134.72	139.72
4-13	134.57	136.71	134.66	9-7	147.21	136.61	140.78
4-20	134.42	135.25	134.58	9-14	147.77	135.19	142.04
4-27	136.08	135.86	134.60	9-21	144.66	136.55	142.85
5-4	135.93	135.92	134.60	9-28	145.44	136.44	143.75
5-11	134.06	134.07	134.60	10-5	145.34	138.07	144.48
5-18	133.92	134.01	134.59	10-12	145.91	138.65	145.21
5-25	134.33	134.10	134.61	10-19	144.34	140.29	145.61
6-1	134.87	134.42	134.66	10-26	146.76	145.27	145.76
6-8	133.94	133.91	134.66	11-2	146.35	143.83	146.01
6-15	135.91	134.54	134.80	11-9	146.73	146.38	146.05
6-22	134.72	134.57	134.81	11-16	144.39	147.21	145.76
6-29	136.61	134.42	135.03	11-23	144.68	147.77	145.46
7-6	135.19	136.08	134.94	11-30	145.07	144.66	145.50
7-13	136.55	135.93	135.01	12-7	145.03	145.44	145.46
7-20	136.44	134.06	135.24	12-14	143.47	145.34	145.27
7-27	138.07	133.92	135.66	12-21	144.49	145.91	145.13
8-3	138.65	134.33	136.09	12-28	145.38	144.34	145.23

Let us say, we will note a change in trend of the index if the figure for any week is 1.40 - 1.50 or more above or below the moving average and in the opposite direction of the previous trend.

At the start of 1968, the index is declining from the top of a bull move so we wait patiently to see if it will violate the moving average to the prescribed extent. Using the weekly compilation, we find this took place on January 22, when the index was 140.94 and the average 142.90.

We also have been keeping weekly prices on four commodities: July soybeans, July wheat, July pork bellies and July cocoa. We examine these prices to see if they, too, are below their 10 week moving averages.

There is only one, wheat. See Table 12. We sell short July wheat at 150 on the opening January 23. We also keep a narrowed eye on the other three commodities and on the index.

Table 12. TEN WEEK MOVING AVERAGES

July 1968 Soybeans				July 1968 Wheat			
1967 Date	**Close**	**Deduct**	**M. A.**	**1967 Date**	**Close**	**Deduct**	**M. A.**
10-23	273.12			10-23	161.00		
10-30	274.12			10-30	159.50		
11-6	274.75			11-6	156.38		
11-13	277.00			11-13	154.87		
11-20	276.00			11-20	154.50		
11-27	276.50			11-27	155.25		
12-4	276.00			12-4	154.00		
12-11	277.62			12-11	153.75		
12-18	278.12			12-18	154.25		
12-22	277.87		276.11	12-22	153.00		155.65
1968				**1968**			
1-2	276.38	273.12	276.43	1-2	149.50	161.00	154.50
1-9	277.25	274.12	276.74	1-9	151.00	159.50	153.65
1-15	279.25	274.75	277.19	1-15	151.87	156.38	153.19
1-22	278.25	277.00	277.32	1-22	149.87	154.87	152.69
1-29	279.38	276.00	277.66	1-29	151.50	154.50	152.39
2-4	278.50	276.50	277.86	2-4	150.12	155.25	151.88
2-13	278.50	276.00	278.11	2-13	151.00	154.00	151.58
2-19	279.25	277.62	278.27	2-19	151.00	153.75	151.31
2-26	278.87	278.12	278.35	2-26	150.50	154.25	150.93
3-4	279.00	277.87	278.46	3-4	151.75	153.00	150.81
3-11	279.38	276.38	278.76	3-11	153.25	149.50	151.18
3-19	277.25	277.25	278.76	3-19	152.38	151.00	151.32

Two weeks later, July cocoa breaks below its moving average to close at 28.06. We sell it short the next morning at 27.78.

On March 19, soybeans break below their moving average so we sell the July delivery short at 277 1/2 the next day, see Table 12.

May 6 finds July pork bellies, too, are in a downtrend. We short these at 36.02 the next day.

Meanwhile, we are watching the index for any sign of a reversal in trend. The index shows no signs of it although it is leveling off in the 135-136 area.

Accordingly, we hold all our short positions until June 28, when we buy them in since July is becoming the cash month and we don't want to hold futures contracts due in that month.

These trades have now resulted in the following profit figures:

Commodity	Bought	Sold	One Contract Gross Profit
Soybeans	266 7/8	277 1/2	$ 531
Wheat	126 5/8	150	1,168
Pork Bellies	29.95	36.02	1,821
Cocoa	25.16	27.78	786
			$4,306

Commissions totaled about $140, so a little under $4,200 could have been made on such a series of trades. Of course, since the trend has not changed, we can now substitute later deliveries for those closed out and, accordingly, we immediately sell short:

November soybeans 256 1/4
December wheat 137 1/4
February pork bellies 34.00
December cocoa 26.52

What happened? As you can see, the index remained quiescent and in an apparent sideways trend until the weekly tabulation of October 7, when it finally penetrated the moving average 136.67 to 134.74.

The next morning we covered our June 28 short sales:

Commodity	Bought	Sold	One Contract Gross Profit
Soybeans	250 5/8	256 1/4	$ 281
Wheat	122 3/4	137 1/4	725
Pork Bellies	33.97	34.00	7
Cocoa	34.91	26.52	(2,517)
			($1,504)

Adding commissions of about $140 results in a loss of $1,644 for this series. The net profit for the two series, which cover only one major move of the index is $2,522. Approximate margin originally was about $3,100.

This situation on cocoa gives us pause. How can we protect ourselves against the commodity which won't follow the index trend? After a good deal of figuring, we decide to make these rules:

> **Any commodity which registers a 300% gross profit on original margin should be liquidated and the profit taken.**
> **Any commodity which shows a loss of all of its original margin should be liquidated and the loss taken.**
> **If it is necessary to put a commodity delivery forward, the accumulated profit or loss should also be put forward and used in the above computations.**

If these rules had been in effect during the last trend, they would not have influenced the January 23-June 28 tabulation. However with wheat margin at $500, soybeans at $600, pork bellies $1,000 and cocoa $1,000, the June 29-October 7 results would have been:

Commodity	Bought	Sold	One Contract Gross Profit
Soybeans	250 5/8	256 1/4	$ 281
Wheat	131 1/2	137 1/4	287
Pork Bellies	30.07	34.00	1,179
Cocoa	32.47	26.52	(1,785)
			($ 38)

Of the four commodities used, three of them hit our limits. Wheat profits totaled $1,500 gross on July 30 and pork bellies $3,000 on August 5, while December cocoa had a net loss of $1,000 on September 6.

Combining the two positions, which were all one downward trend of the index, showed a net profit of $3,988 after commissions of $280.

Now, for the next move! On October 7, we examine the moving averages of our four commodities and find both pork bellies and cocoa were above their averages. Acting on this, we bought March pork bellies at 34.30 and March cocoa at 36.00 the next morning, October 8.

Both soybeans and wheat went into uptrends on the next weekly compilation, so we bought March soybeans at 259 and March wheat at 131 1/4 on the morning of October 15.

Late in the month, we ran into trouble on our pork bellies and we finally had to sell them out at 31.00 on November 4 for a loss of $999 plus commission.

Our cocoa, on the other hand, proved itself a junior grade bonanza. Our original margin was profitably doubled and then on December 11, we sold out at 46.60 on the opening (up from a 45.60 close) for a profit of $3,180 less commission.

The wheat and soybean contracts remained pedestrian, moving along with the index but never near the high or low points of our sell-out rules.

The index continued to advance until January 20, 1969, when it turned down. We immediately sold out our remaining long positions:

Commodity	Bought	Sold	One Contract Gross Profit
Soybeans	259	263 3/4	$ 237
Wheat	131 1/4	134 1/8	143
Pork Bellies	34.30	31.00	(999)
Cocoa	36.00	46.60	3,180
			$2,561

Commissions total about $140 and should be deducted from the gross.

Examining the record of the four commodities, we find our new rules saved us a good deal of money. While pork bellies did recover from their low point to open at 33.42 on January 21, cocoa declined sharply and was selling at a mere 36.80 on January 21. So, although we would have made back about two-thirds of our belly loss, we would also have sacrificed almost all of our cocoa profit if we had waited to sell out until the index turned down.

Let us continue our examination of the index's trends. The trend turned down, as we have recorded, on January 20. We will, therefore, sell the September delivery of wheat, soybeans and cocoa and the August delivery of pork bellies.

On January 20, wheat and cocoa are already in downtrends according to our weekly price averages for the last ten weeks, so we sell them on the morning of January 21; September wheat at 135 5/8 and September cocoa at 38.50. September soybeans join the downtrend on March 10 and August bellies on April 8.

Our cocoa and bellies rallied to the point of margin exhaustion and we closed them out at the stop loss points. The index trend reversed itself on July 7 so we covered our two remaining positions the next morning.

Commodity	Bought	Sold	One Contract Gross Profit
Soybeans	246 1/2	245 1/4	$ (63)
Wheat	131 3/8	135 5/8	212
Pork Bellies	38.80	35.47	(999)
Cocoa	41.83	38.50	(999)
			($1,849)

Commissions of about $140 should be added to this total.

Of the four commodities we are using, only wheat is not in an uptrend on July 7, so we buy the March deliveries of the other three on the morning of July 8. We have to wait until September 3 to buy March wheat when it finally goes into an uptrend. The index turns down on December 22, 1969.

Commodity	Bought	Sold	One Contract Gross Profit
Soybeans	242 1/2	245	$ 125
Wheat	136 1/8	146	493
Pork Bellies	36.50	46.50	3,000
Cocoa	39.38	38.42	(288)
			$3,330

Commissions are now figured at the new rates and total $165 which should be deducted from this profit. Pork bellies were the good performers in this series reaching our 300 percent of margin figure on December 4.

Since the index has now turned down, we examine our four commodities and find all except wheat are in a downtrend too. We sell May cocoa, pork bellies and soybeans on the opening December 23. Wheat finally turns down on January 12, so we sell that the next day. The index continues its downward trend until April 27, 1970, when it turns up. The results of this last move are quite interesting:

Commodity	Bought	Sold	One Contract Gross Profit
Soybeans	267	255	$ (600)
Wheat	150 1/2	142 1/4	(412)
Pork Bellies	46.15	42.82	(999)
Cocoa	27.92	37.92	3,000
			$ 989

Three of our four commodities hit our trading limits of 300 percent of margin profit or 100 percent of margin loss. The winner was cocoa, the two 100 percent losers were soybeans and bellies with wheat nearly there. Again, $165 commissions should be deducted from the gain.

We reverse our positions again and buy January soybeans, August pork bellies and December wheat on the morning of April 28, 1970. Cocoa does not go into an uptrend until July 6. We buy the March delivery the next morning. The index remains upward until November 16, 1970. We sell out our remaining positions the next morning:

Commodity	Bought	Sold	One Contract Gross Profit
Soybeans	265 3/4	304 (opg)	$1,912
Wheat	150	171 1/4	1,062

Commodity	Bought	Sold	One Contract Gross Profit
Pork Bellies	42.07	39.30	(997)
Cocoa	27.25	28.00	225
			$2,202

Commissions of $165 should be deducted from this total.

This was an interesting series. Wheat at one time was within 5/8 cent of being a 100 percent loss and cocoa rose to 36.80 on September 8, or within 45 points of a $3,000 profit. Beans were full of fireworks and easily achieved their 300 percent of margin objective on July 13 when they opened at 304, which gave us a little added profit. Their margin was raised during this move but it did not affect our original deposit of $600.

We now have used the Dow Jones Commodity Futures Index as a guide for about three years in these ghost transactions. In that time, based on our 10 week moving average method, it has forecast six trends. A rough summary of our results using our revised rules has been:

January 22, 1968 to October 8, 1968	$3,988
October 8, 1968 to January 21, 1969	2,421
January 21, 1969 to July 8, 1969	(1,989)
July 8, 1969 to December 23, 1969	3,165
December 23, 1969 to April 28, 1970	824
April 28, 1970 to November 17, 1970	2,037
	$10,446

While no bonanza, these results are certainly impressive and do much to back my argument that commodities are a better investment than stocks. In three years of purely mechanical adherence to this method, we have made over 10,000 ghost dollars net. Using the original margin of $3,100 as a starting point, we have made over 337 percent on our capital or at an overall rate of almost 113 per year.

I do not know what the results would have been had we used any other commodities but I suspect that they would have been about the same. After combining the original and carried forward trades into one, we had the following gross profit and trade results:

Commodity	Gross Profit	Profit Trades	Loss Trades	300% Profit	100% Loss
Soybeans	$2,423	4	2	1	1
Wheat	2,953	5	1	1	0

Commodity	Gross Profit	Profit Trades	Loss Trades	300% Profit	100% Loss
Pork Bellies	2,006	2	4	2	4
Cocoa	4,119	3	3	2	2
	$11,501				
Commissions	1,055				
	$10,446				

This compilation is very interesting. We have had only four more profit trades than losses yet we have made over 337 percent in three years. Pork bellies were the neck-or-nothing performer. Perhaps the fluctuations on these are too great for this type of method even though they did show a profit. A cyclical commodity is handicapped if the index trend is against the cyclical trend.

For those who wish to follow or experiment with this method, I now submit the following rules:

1. Wait for a change of 1.40 or more against the 10 week moving average of the Dow Jones Commodity Futures Index.

2. Make a commitment in at least four actively traded commodities the next morning *if* they are in the same new trend as the index. If any are not, wait until their individual 10 week averages show them to be in such a trend.

3. Try to use futures which are at least six months from first delivery date. Put them forward if they are about to become deliverable and the index trend has not changed.

4. Reverse your position the morning after a weekly change in the index trend.

5. Take profits on individual commodities at 300 percent of original margin on that commodity.

6. Take losses of 100 percent of original margin on that commodity.

7. Meet all margin calls during the trend.

25

HOW TO FIND TAX AND TAX STRADDLES ADVANTAGES*

Commodity trading has several Federal income tax advantages over stocks. Briefly, they may be itemized as follows:

1. The 30 day "wash sale" rule does not apply to commodity loss trades.
2. Long and short term gains and losses can be planned somewhat at the speculator's will, depending on his yearly tax situation.

When you sell a stock at a loss and want to rebuy it, you must wait over 30 days before doing so. If you do not, the sale becomes a wash sale and is disallowed as a deduction by the I.R.S. This is not so in commodities.

The important reason for this difference is in its threat to the liquidity of the commodity markets. While there are roughly 5,000 stocks traded daily on the various exchanges and over-the-counter markets, there are usually only a few deliveries of the various commodity futures.

Suppose you have a number of wheat-corn spreads outstanding in which you have bought July, September, December, March and May wheat and sold a proportionate number of corn deliveries. The spreads are working out, you have a loss on the wheat side but a bigger profit on your short corn. You decide to cash the spreads in, selling out your long wheat at a loss and buying in the short corn at a profit. If the 30 day rule applied, you would not be allowed to buy any more of those deliveries of wheat for over 30 days since you want to count your wheat losses against your corn profits. Multiply *you* by thousands of others who had taken wheat losses in the course of daily trading and you can see the threat to the basic need for having commodity markets at all, the availability of speculators to assume the trades of the hedgers who produce, store or use wheat.

This, I hope, explains the missing 30 day rule in commodities.

As in stocks, however, the speculator should be aware of the great tax difference between long and short term gains and losses. This has become even more important with the enactment of the 1969 tax law which allows only a deduction of 50 percent of net long term losses.

Long term gains and losses are taken on *all purchases* held over six months.

Short term gains and losses are taken on *all short sales and on all purchases* held six months or less.

---

* There have been several recent and unfavorable interpretations by the I.R.S. of "riskless" tax straddles, especially butterfly straddles. Consult your tax man before entering any commodity tax straddles.

Only $1,000 of net capital losses may be deducted from ordinary income for any one year. These can be all short term or 50 percent of long term or a combination of the two. Here is an example:

> Ordinary income $10,000
> Short term capital loss (STCL) 400
> Long term capital loss (LTCL) 2,500

This would result in an adjusted gross income of $9,000 computed as follows:

> Ordinary income $10,000
> STCL—deducted in full before
>   LTCL is applied $400
> LTCL—deducted one-half but only
>   to the extent that the combined
>   deduction of STCL and LTCL does
>   not exceed $1,000 600   1,000
> Adjusted gross income . . . . $ 9,000

The carryover to the next year is computed as follows:

	STCL	LTCL
Current year loss	$ 400	$2,500
Deducted from ordinary income . . .	(400)	(600)
For long term loss, an amount equal to the amount deducted from ordinary income		(600)
Carryover to next year	$ 0	$1,300

The deduction from ordinary income is $1,000 ($400 short term loss + $600 long term loss). When both long and short term losses are present, the short term loss is deducted first. The long term loss carryover is $2,500 − $1,200 = $1,300.

Note that 1/2 of the long term loss is lost forever as a deduction unless it can be applied against capital gain that year.

I hastily say, you should never go into any capital loss or gains situation without the advice and counsel of your tax man. There may be other options than tax straddles open to you.

Tax men apart, however, you can see the great financial advantages of taking short term rather than long term losses. If you have a commodity loss that is going to go long term, switch it to another delivery before it becomes a long term loss. That way, you can take the loss at 100 percent and still, usually, maintain your comparative position.

Another program which may prove of interest to you and your tax man is the "Tax Straddle."

Tax straddles are usually used to negate a short term gain and turn it into a long term profit which, of course, is usually taxed at a lower rate.

How might this be done under the 1969 law which covers the years from 1970?

It is June 1, 1971 and you come to me with a problem. You are a married man and you have just made a very nice capital gain of $45,000. Unfortunately, it is short term. You also estimate that your 1971 earned taxable income, after exemptions and deductions, will be $50,000. These two items will total $95,000, which will result in a tax of approximately $42,180.

Tax on earned taxable income of $50,000 . . . . $17,060
Additional tax on total taxable income of $95,000   25,120
                                                            $42,180

This figures out to be over 44 percent tax on your $95,000. Whew!

You'd love to pay only the 25 percent long term capital gains tax on that $45,000. If you could convert that item to long term, it would reduce your tax bill from $42,180 to $28,310, a savings of $13,870.

	$50,000 + $45,000 of SHORT term gain	$50,000 + $45,000 of LONG term gain
Tax on first $50,000 . . .	$17,060	$17,060
Tax on next $45,000 . . .	25,120	11,250
	$42,180	$28,310

You should note that long term gains in amounts over $50,000 are taxed at the rate of 35 percent for the taxable year of 1972 and any year thereafter. This is on the amount of the gain over the first $50,000. This provision does not affect our present computation.

Also, over and above this long term capital gains tax, a special "preference" tax of 10 percent is levied on 1/2 of long term capital gains to the extent they exceed the taxpayer's regular tax for the year plus $30,000.

This provision does not affect our figuring since your tax for the year will be $28,310, if we can get that $45,000 into the long term category. Adding $28,310 and $30,000 = $58,310. As 1/2 of your long term gain of $45,000 is $22,500, the sum of $58,310 exceeds it so no preference tax is due.

However, if your tax plus $30,000 had been $58,310 and 1/2 your long term capital gain had been $60,000, then an additional preference tax of $169 would have been due:

$$\$60,000 - 58,310 = \$1,690$$
$$\$1,690 + 10\% \quad = \quad 169$$

To get back to our problem. What about converting this short term gain to long term and saving all those tax dollars?

I get out a few charts and attempt to find a commodity which has been volatile and whose delivery months run up and down pretty much in unison. Copper looks like a good one at this time. It has wide ranges and not too much change in the relative position of the delivery months. If one goes up 50 points in a day, the others usually go up 40 to 60 points.

We start to figure. Copper price changes are at the rate of $250 per 1 cent of change. If a delivery of copper were to change 5 cents between now and December 31, it would total $1,250 per contract. Thirty-five contracts times $1,250 would equal $43,750, just about the amount you need.

You decide to buy 35 contracts of May copper and sell 35 contracts of July copper to set up a tax straddle.

Long Term	**Short Term**
June 28: Bought May @ 50.00¢	June 28: Sold July @ 51.00¢

Now what can happen?

Example 1. On December 31, copper is up 4 cents. You sell out your long May for a long term capital gain of $35,000 (4 x $250 x 35). You also buy in your short July for a short term capital loss of $35,000. You have succeeded in converting $35,000 of your short term gain to long term. Your tax situation is now:

$$\text{Tax on first } \$60,000 \dots \dots \dots \dots \$22,300$$
$$\text{Tax on LTCG } 35,000 \dots \dots \dots \dots \underline{8,750}$$
$$\$31,050$$

This represents a savings of about $11,130 in your tax bill which would have totaled $42,180 without the benefits of your tax spread. Of course, commissions and interest on your margin money have to be deducted from the above savings but I doubt if these would total over $2,000.

Example 2. On December 27, copper is down 4 cents from your two straddle prices. You sell out your long May and take a short term loss of $35,000. You simultaneously replace your May with long September to reestablish your straddle position. You use September because you will have to have enough time to get over six months of ownership established. By July 1, copper is up around 7 cents from the December 27 price. You liquidate both sides of your straddle.

Long Term	**Short Term**
June 28: Bought May @50.00¢	June 28: Sold July @ 51.00¢
Dec. 27: Sold May @46.00¢	
Dec. 27: Bought Sept. @52.00¢	
July 1: Sold Sept. @ 59.00¢	July 1: Bought July @ 54.00¢

Now, let's see how all this has affected your tax picture.

When you sold out your long May copper on December 27, you took a loss of $35,000 which would apply against most of that $45,000 of short term capital gain you had. Note, it would not have mattered if you had sold out at the same price on December 29, thus, creating a long term capital loss. In any compilation, long term capital losses are applied against short term gains, dollar for dollar and vice versa. It is only when one exceeds the other you have to start figuring.

In this case, you still have $10,000 of short term gain outstanding at the end of the year. Therefore, you have a net income of $60,000 which includes $50,000 earned income and $10,000 short term gain.

Tax on first $52,000	$18,060
53% on next $8,000	4,240
Tax due . . .	$22,300

However, that was last year. You now have this year's taxes to consider. When you liquidated the spread on July 1, you got a long term gain on the September copper of $61,250 (7 x $250 x 35 = $61,250). You also got a short term loss on the July copper (3 x $250 x 35 = $26,250). Deducting $26,250 from $61,250 leaves a long term gain of $35,000.

Assuming your earned net income after deductions and exemptions this year will be about $50,000, you will have the following tax picture:

Tax on first $44,000	$14,060
50% on next $6,000	3,000
25% on LTCG $35,000	8,750
Tax due . . .	$25,810

If you had not had the long term capital gain but instead had the $35,000 short term, your tax picture on $85,000 income would have been:

Tax on first $76,000	$31,020
58% on next $9,000	5,220
Tax due . .	$36,240

As I have said before, these examples do not include either commissions on the straddles nor loss of interest on your margin deposit. You should have a good idea of what these will be before going into any straddles.

In these two examples, I have given you some rather idealized situations which had the luck to work out to the extent that almost 80 percent of the objective was realized. We wanted to get $45,000 long term and we actually got $35,000 which was a very good percentage. Usually, they don't work out so neatly. Sometimes, you get in a long downtrend and continually take profits on the short side of your straddle. These are short term, of course, and the losses which you take on the long side are short term, too. Anyway, it is a good plan to see that they are. Even if these profits and losses are equal, after commissions, you still have not accomplished your objective of establishing a long term profit. If you persevere, the market will eventually turn up. You can only hope it will do so before the commissions dollar you to death.

Another thing to remember, sometimes the point difference between the months will widen or narrow, often to your disadvantage. That is why I always try to use adjoining months. Metals are not seasonal or cyclical so they tend to run pretty much in unison, especially adjoining months, March to May, July to September and even closer if you can get them. The nearest month should usually be the buy side of your straddle, so pick one that will give you six months *before* first delivery day. By doing this, you will eliminate the necessity of having to pay double commissions on the sell side of your straddle.

If you were to buy May and sell March in October, you would have to buy in the short March and sell September before you got a long term profit on May, perhaps sometime in April.

Of course, you would do this on or about December 31, if the March had gone up enough to give you a short term loss. But if the market went down there would be no necessity for it and you would have had to pay extra commissions just to put your short March forward to September during the first two months of the next year. All this could have been avoided if you had sold short July instead of March.

Some traders like to "butterfly" their straddles. They might buy May and September and sell twice as much of July, in the middle. Being long one May and one September and short 2 July gives them a little more latitude and also may save them a commission if their spread hasn't worked out by May and they have to sell out the May and put it forward to September or December.

Others like to protect themselves by only putting on spreads which are the same crop and near the carrying charge. For instance, the carrying charge on wheat is about 1 1/2 cents per bushel per month. If March and May wheat are about 4 cents apart, May over March, you estimate such a ratio may hold or even narrow slightly in normal markets. However, watch yourself when spreading anything grown or raised. Don't go into different crop years March wheat vs. July wheat for example, unless you are very sure of your position.

The tax computations I have given here are only approximate and your own individual situation should be rigorously checked by you and your tax consultant before entering the market.

My advice on tax straddles has been right about as many times as it has been wrong. The usual complaint is that the commodity chosen does not move up or down enough to establish the proper amount of gains or losses. Occasionally, the moves, if they do not lose money, will barely cover commissions which is fine for the broker but not much help to the customer.

Here are a few ideas gathered from experience with tax straddles:

1. Be sure the game is worth the candle. The amount saved in taxes should be enough to warrant the cost and risk of the straddle.

2. Pick a commodity which has been volatile the last three months.

3. Pick a commodity in which the spread difference between the delivery months has remained fairly constant.

4. Use adjoining months for the straddle, the nearest being the buy side of your straddle.

5. Be *sure* you can get in six months and one day on your buy side before the first delivery date. Check this.

6. Unless the amount to be saved is large, don't renew your straddle more than once. Your commissions and interest on your margin money may be too high in relation to the amount you are trying to save.

7. Do not let your losses go long term.

8. When placing your straddle or changing deliveries, *always do so simultaneously,* preferably on the same order. In this way, you will usually get special straddle commissions which are lower than the regular rate on most exchanges. Some, however, won't let you switch deliveries at the special commission rates, others will. Find out about this before you make your commitments. It can save you money.

9. Consult your tax man before you do anything about a *commodity* tax straddle. If he doesn't know about them, find one who does.

10. Good luck!

26

HOW TO FIND ADDITIONAL INFORMATION

Probably nowhere in a speculator's world is accurate information so essential to success and so hard to obtain as in the commodity markets.

Gossip? Yes, it abounds. Opinions? Everyone has an opinion. But reliable information? It is usually either out-of-date or unavailable, neither of which is going to do you any good.

Thus, the speculator is forced to build his own opinion based on the information which everyone else knows and on which the market action has presumably already been taken. A rather frustrating situation.

It is this very lack of reliable information that drives the speculator to use all the seasonal, cyclical, mechanical and computer methods already described in these pages. If he can't analyze the data he has, well, let the market try to tell him what it all means.

Yet, the big money in the commodity markets is almost always made by astute persons who take the information available to all, make their own interpretation of it, make and triple-margin their commitment and sit back until the market comes to the moment of truth they have foreseen, which is their moment to take a large profit.

This is an example. Most speculators are aware of the salad oil scandal which occurred in late 1963 when a certain gentleman tried to control those markets through some very intricate hanky-panky. When his efforts collapsed, soybean oil dropped 325 points ($1,950 per contract) in four days to a price of 7.05 cents a lb. It quickly rebounded to about 8.25 cents but then drifted lower over the years to a price of about 7.00 cents in the summer of 1969.

At this point, one of my customers called me and said, "Soybean oil is selling at less than it did the day of the big market slump in 1963. We must be near the low point in its price. Buy forty contracts."

He profited handsomely on the subsequent rise during 1970 to over 11 cents.

My point is that he was not operating on inside information but on his own interpretation of information available to everyone.

Another such situation developed during the tremendous rise in pork belly prices during December, 1965. A customer called and said any time bacon got above $1.20 a pound in the stores, his wife quit buying it. It was now $1.29 per pound and he felt it was wise to sell belly futures short. He sold at 45.00 cents and at 47.00 cents and was twice called for margin when the price hit 50.00 and 52.00. He put up the additional margin, still convinced he was right and bacon consumption would drop sharply. A month later, the price was back to about 46.00 and in another month, he was able to cover his short sales at about 42.00 for a good profit.

Here, again, was a case of a trader having information available to all and enough money to sit back and wait for the market to finally respond to that information.

Of course, if this type of trading was sure-fire, there would be a lot more of it so I'd better review a case that did not work out.

Early in 1969, a good customer called and said, "I notice July wheat is selling at a premium of only 12 cents over July corn. That's a very narrow margin, sometimes in the past it has been over 70 cents and I can't remember any time it has been this low. Put on a spread for me; buy July wheat and sell July corn."

The spread was placed. Incidentally, I agreed with his analysis. Going back over the years, I could find no cases in the last 20 years when the difference between wheat and corn had been that close. It looked as if it must widen.

What happened? On June 29, the last day we dared hold July wheat, the spread had closed up to a difference of 2 1/2 cents and we took a loss of 10 cents per bushel on our transaction. I urged him to carry the spread forward that day to March wheat and March corn at about an 11 cents difference but he had had enough and said, "You say this hasn't happened in 20 years! Well, why did it have to happen to me?"

In a few months, the March spread had widened to 26 cents and by the end of February, 1970, it was about 31 cents. Had my customer had the nerve and the money, he could have profited by his analysis of the situation instead of losing a lot of money.

I have given you these three illustrations to show that while your information may be correct, you often have to sit awhile before the market begins to agree with you and you *must* have the money to ride out untoward, temporary reverses—and some that aren't so darned temporary!

Now, where do you get such information as is available? There are three or four places:

The United States Department of Agriculture announcements which are official government estimates, the "private" crop reports on grains, the more reliable subscription services and your brokerage firm's own analysis of the situation.

I would not want to rate these as to reliability. Sometimes, the government estimates are off due to conditions which have occurred since the date of the estimate. Many times, the other services can make an astute judgement of the situation and every once in awhile, your broker's firm will come up with a different—and winning—analysis.

Your job, of course, is to sift through all this information and filter out the 99 percent chaff to get at the 1 percent kernel of profitable truth.

Many people go with the government's figures just because they have faith in the mysterious "they" who apparently run the show. A little analysis of how the government's reports are arrived at and released may now be in order.

Voluntary mail samplings are the keystone of the government effort. These samplings fall into four categories:

1. Regular monthly reporters who receive a general crop and livestock questionnaire the first of each month.

2. Farmers who report for their individual farms in March on intentions to plant and in June on crop acreages for harvest and in late fall on acreage harvested and production from that harvest.

3. Farmers in many states who receive individual farm questionnaire cards from rural mail carriers three times each year. In June and December, they are asked about livestock and in October about crop acreages.

4. Special purpose samplings used in forecasts and estimates of livestock products and other products of which an adequate sampling cannot be obtained by general purpose mailing.

Mail questionnaires are also used for other purposes of agricultural reporting.

Of course, not all farmers get a questionnaire. Probability sampling in which certain farmers in certain areas are used is the mode of making estimates just as the television networks do on election night when they predict a winner hours in advance of the final count.

Enumerative surveys are conducted by the government twice a year. In these, trained interviewers visit selected farms in each area and secure the necessary information. The first survey is in June and puts a major emphasis on crop acreage. It also includes livestock numbers, farm labor and wages. It covers about 25,000 resident farms including about 4,000 extremely large livestock and poultry farms.

The second survey is made in December and only covers a sub-sample of the farms visited in June. The main purpose is to estimate livestock inventories and production but it also includes questions as to acres of all seeded crops, farm labor and wage rates.

Another major government program is the "objective yield" survey of crops. In this, enumerators repeatedly visit sample plots in a sample of fields during the growing season to obtain accurate quantitative data by counting and measuring of plants, blooms and the size and weight of the yield.

All these probability sample surveys are then processed on computers in advance of the "lockup" release date. Survey indications for crops in which there is a speculative interest on the exchanges are printed out in a scrambled code, placed in sealed envelopes and held in a special security lockbox until the morning of the lockup.

On the day of the lockup, three crop reporting members and a representative of the Secretary of Agriculture go to a locked room containing the security lockbox. Just to add tinsel, they are accompanied by an armed guard.

The Secretary of the Crop Reporting Board has one key to the box and the representative of the Secretary of Agriculture has the other. They unlock the box and remove its contents. Then, the members of the board, accompanied by the armed guard, take the reports to the lockup area where the crop report will be prepared.

The lockup area is a series of offices which can be locked off from the rest of the building. In this area, all window blinds have been closed and sealed and all telephones disconnected. The guard, now augmented by others, is stationed outside the locked doors.

Within the lockup areas, the speculative commodity reports are removed from the box, decoded and handed around. Each board member makes his own estimate and interpretation of the data with the chairman resolving any disagreements. After this, suitable computer print-outs of the determinations are made, the final report is mimeographed and distributed to the press at 3:00 p.m. that same day.

While all the above seems to rule out hanky-panky, a little mystery that happened about six or seven years ago still nags at my mind. At that time, the government was said to be quite worried about the early release of speculative information to certain persons. Nothing was ever said in public yet the trade sensed that something was cooking. Too many markets were responding in advance to the later news in these reports.

So, one report day, the soybean market had quite an advance. Sure enough, the report came out with a lower estimate of soybean production than had been anticipated by the general public. The bulls who had followed the day's advance and bought beans were happy. But, the next day, the government corrected its report to show many more soybeans than the previous estimate. Blandly, it laid the blame on a "clerical error" which had omitted the crop data, I believe, from the state of Minnesota!

The government results, it should be emphasized, are only estimates. Obviously, no government agency can count every bushel of wheat growing in the fields nor can it adjust its total quickly for the local conditions which may affect the crop after the estimate date.

Besides the estimates, the USDA publishes much additional information and, at stated intervals through the year, it sends out pamphlets outlining the whole situation called, appropriately, *The Wheat Situation, The Fats and Oils Situation* and several others. These pamphlets contain a wealth of information and are available by mail. Get your name on the list to receive those in which you are interested by writing the USDA in Washington, D.C., asking for its list of publications. You're paying for this service; you might as well use it.

The Commodity Research Bureau, 140 Broadway, New York, N.Y., 10005 is the largest of the private subscription services. It publishes three main sources of information. Its weekly *Futures Market Service,* known as the "blue sheet," deals in factual estimates and ideas; its weekly chart service is much used by devotees of that exotic art and its computer service has been in operation for almost a decade, first as a weekly and now on a daily basis. Your local broker probably subscribes to some or all of these services.

Lastly, there is your own brokerage firm's fount of knowledge. This can be very good or plain terrible and you will have to acquire enough experience with your own particular firm to judge its quality.

Do not disdain and do not wholly believe any sources of information. The best you can do is to review all carefully and make an educated estimate as to their accuracy and, more important, as to the eventual effect on the market.

Glossary of Terms

The commodity markets, like every other business, have their own verbal shorthand. I have listed only those terms which you may encounter in the normal course of your trading activities.

Basis. The difference between the price of a future and the cash price. If July future is selling 2 cents over cash, the basis is "two cents under July."

Bid and Ask. The prices at which a commodity may be bought and sold at a certain moment on the floor of the exchange. You can sell at the bid price and buy at the asked price.

Buy. You want to take a long position in a commodity.

Buy-in. You want to buy-in all or part of a short position that you already have. Never say, "Sell out my short wheat." Do say, "Buy-in my short wheat."

Carrying charge. Usually refers to warehouse charges, insurance, inspection and other charges incurred when you own cash commodities. Never get entangled in this mess.

C.F.T.C. The Commodity Futures Trading Commission, an agency of the U.S. Government which supervises and regulates all U.S. Commodity Exchanges.

Contract. The unit of a commodity that makes one regular trading unit. Wheat is 5,000 bushels, potatoes 50,000 lbs., cattle 40,000 lbs., etc.

Corner. When one or more parties at interest have bought up the available supply of a commodity and thus can set the price which those who have previously sold short must cover their contracts. Illegal on all exchanges.

Cover. The cancellation of a short position. You would say, "I'm covering my shorts in sugar," when you give the order to buy-in your short position.

Crop year. Like the automobile industry, the commodities of the country do not have calendar years in the introduction of new models. The wheat crop year begins July 1, corn with the December delivery, hogs on October 1, etc. Find out the crop year, if any, on your particular commodity.

Cyclical trend. Applied only to those commodities which are grown, used and sold every day, such as eggs, hogs, cattle, porkbellies.

Delivery. The tender and receipt of the actual commodity. Ugh!

First notice day. The first day on which delivery notices can be given to the unsuspecting, therefore foolish, trader.

G.T.C. Good until cancelled or open order.

Government reports. Any of the many reports issued from time to time by the U.S.D.A. or other government agency concerning the progress of a crop, its consumption, price supports or other material information.

Hedge. Buying or selling futures against the ownership or prospective ownership or consumption of the actual commodity.

Loan prices. The prices at which producers may obtain government loans on their crops. If, after a specified period the loans are not paid off with interest and storage charges, the amount of the commodity pledged for the loan then becomes the property of the government.

Long. You have a net position showing more open purchases than open sales in a commodity.

Margin. Your earnest money deposited with the broker as a guarantee of payment of your account.

Margin call. A demand for additional funds to guarantee the payment of your account.

Market letter. The opinion of one of many brokerage firms or individuals as to the future course of the market.

Minimum price change. The smallest price change which can occur between prices on a commodity. Wheat is 1/8 cent or $6.25 per 5,000 bushel contract. Pork bellies is 2 1/2 cents or $9.00 per contract.

Open interest. The number of unliquidated purchases and sales but never their combined total. You might re-read my chapter on Open Interest.

Pit. The octagonal, stepped platform on the Chicago Board of Trade floor upon which traders stand while executing futures trades.

Pyramid. A method of using profits to add to your position without the deposit of additional margin.

Range. The difference between the high and low prices for any given period. *Daily range, opening range, closing range*.

Ring. A circular platform on the trading floor of many exchanges upon which brokers stand while executing orders.

Seasonal trend. Applied usually to those commodities which are only harvested once a year: wheat, corn, oats, soybeans, etc.

Sell-out. To sell a previously purchased contract of a commodity.

Sell short. To sell a contract of a commodity that you do not own. However, you may own a contract of May wheat and still sell short July wheat since this is not the same contract as the one you own.

Short. You have a net position showing an excess of open sales over open purchases in a commodity.

Spot price. The cash price of a commodity which varies with locality.

Stop loss order or **Stop order**. An order which is executed only if the market reaches the level mentioned in the order. Read my chapter on orders.

Straddle or **Spread**. The purchase of one delivery of a commodity and the simultaneous sale of another delivery or commodity.

U.S.D.A. United Stares Department of Agriculture. The department which issues all the federal government's reports on the commodities grown or produced in this country. It has general authority over all regulated commodities, their exchanges, trading, loan values, crop allocations, marketing methods, quality specifications and the like. A huge agency, half "pork barrel" and half dedicated, capable people trying to do a good job under almost impossible laws.

Miscellaneous:

Bot. When used means bought.

Cwt. Hundred weight.

Dates. When used to show past performance, dates were as specified or usually the nearest date to it commensurate with consistency.

M. Thousand.

Prices: Unless specified otherwise, these are usually closing prices.

Basic Sources of Information

Gold, Gerald, *Modern Commodity Futures Trading.* New York, N.Y., Commodity Research Bureau, Inc., 1968, 5th ed.

Smith, Adam, *The Money Game,* New York, Random House, 1967.

Edwards, Robert D. and John Magee, *Technical Analysis of Stock Trends.* Springfield, Mass., John Magee, 1966, 5th ed.

Chicago Board of Trade, 141 W. Jackson Blvd., Chicago, Ill. and the *Chicago Mercantile Exchange,* 110 N. Franklin St., Chicago, Ill. *Yearbooks* are published by both exchanges. These are available at reasonable prices on a first-come first-served basis late in April of each year and contain detailed data on the high, low and close of every commodity traded on their exchanges during the past year. Much additional information is also given concerning the statistical situation of the markets. Place your orders early, as the yearbooks are quickly sold out.

Films. If you are interested in being educated via the cinema, the Chicago Board of Trade has produced a very successful film called *The Speculators.* If you can get together a group of 25 or more persons, the Board is glad to loan you a print. Write for details. The Chicago Mercantile Exchange also has several films available and you can write to that exchange for information about them.

Commodity Research Bureau, Inc., 140 Broadway, New York 10005, has several publications.
Daily: *Computer Trend Analyzer.*
Weekly: *The Futures Market Service* and the *Commodity Chart Analysis.*
Annually: *Yearbook.*
Miscellaneous: A Guide to Commodity Price Forecasting.
Write to the Bureau for prices.

Hedging Highlights, pamphlet, Chicago Board of Trade, 141 W. Jackson Blvd., Chicago, Ill.

Morgan, Rogers & Roberts, Inc., 150 Broadway, New York, N.Y. 10038. The company has a book available on point and figure charting, also a plentitude of other material including charts and guides. Write for information and prices.

The United States Department of Agriculture, Washington, D.C. 20250. The department publishes many pamphlets concerning the various commodities grown or produced in the country. Write for its list.

The Wall Street Journal (New York), 30 Broad St. You can subscribe for three or six months or by the year. Clip the commodity section and keep it in a yearly folder. Invaluable for research work.

Your brokerage firm. All the large firms have pamphlets and reports concerning commodities and commodity trading. Ask for them.

All Commodity Exchanges publish pamphlets on the commodities they handle.

Your broker can give you the name and address of any particular exchange. Indeed, he might have these little pamphlets in his file. If he doesn't write the secretary of the exchange in question.

INDEX

INDEX

Spreading, advantages of (cont.):
  history, researching, 71-72
  illustrations for, 79-80
  out-of-line, 73-74
  prices, examining before placing spread,
    76-78
  seasonal, 71
"Stop" order, meaning of, 42
"Straddling," advantages of, 70-78
(see also "Spreading, advantages of")
Substitution, conversion and, how to use, 81-86
  alfalfa, 85
  corn, 84
  Corn-Hog Ratio, 85-86
  cottonseed oil, 84
  "m.h." market, 83
  milo, 85
  oats, 84-85
  "reverse conversion" spread, 82
  soybeans, 81-84
    meal, 85
  wheat, 84
Sum of the averages method, 126-127

T

Tax and tax straddles, how find advantages,
  152-158
  advantages, two, 152
  "butterflying" straddles, 157
  ideas about, 158
  long and short term gains and losses,
    152-257
  30-day rule, 152
  "Tax straddle," 154
Technical Analysis of Stock Trends, 97n
10 day average, meaning of, 139
The Wall Street Journal, 107, 127
The Wheat Situation, the Fats and Oils Situations, 162
30 day rule, nonapplicability of to commodity
  loss trades, 152
Time, elimination of by point and figure, 98
Time, limitation of on orders, 41

Trading, using mechanical methods of, 107-118
  for pork bellies, 108-118
  purpose of, 107
  types, 107
Trading limits, daily, table of, 50-51
Trading Volume, how to use, 137-140
  change total, meaning of, 139
  11th day deduct, meaning of, 139
  pork bellies futures table, 137-138
  10 day average, meaning of, 139
Trend, finding as purpose of bar charting, 87
Triangle, formation of on bar chart, 90-94
  "Downward Slanting," 92, 94
  "Simple triangle," 90-92
  "Upward Slanting," 91-92
Triple averaging, 126-127
  sugar method tabulation, 128-136

U

United States Department of Agriculture, 160
Unregulated commodities, 28
"Upward slanting triangle," formation of on
  bar chart, 91-92
U.S. Hatchery Production chart, 67

V

Varying margins, reasons for, 33-34
Volume, recording on bar chart, 97
Volume, trading, how to use, 137-140
  change total, meaning of, 139
  11th day deduct, meaning of, 139
  pork bellies future table, 137-138
  10 day average, meaning of, 139
Voluntary mail samplings as keystone in government effort, 160-161

W

Wall Street Journal, 107, 127
"Wash sale" rule, nonapplicability of to commodity loss trades, 152
Wheat, 84
Wheat, computer record on, 122-123
Winnipeg Grain Exchange, 76